PIANO/VOCAL

LOW VOICE

# FIRST 50
# BROADWAY SONGS

## YOU SHOULD SING

Andrew Lloyd Webber™ is a trademark owned by Andrew Lloyd Webber.

ISBN 978-1-4950-7462-2

7777 W. BLUEMOUND RD. P.O. BOX 13819 MILWAUKEE, WI 53213

Visit Hal Leonard Online at
www.halleonard.com

# CONTENTS

# ANY DREAM WILL DO
## from JOSEPH AND THE AMAZING TECHNICOLOR® DREAMCOAT

Music by ANDREW LLOYD WEBBER
Lyrics by TIM RICE

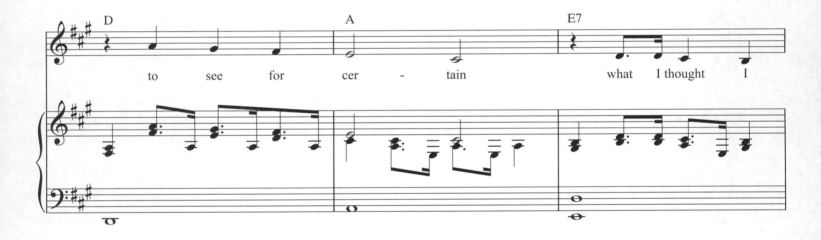

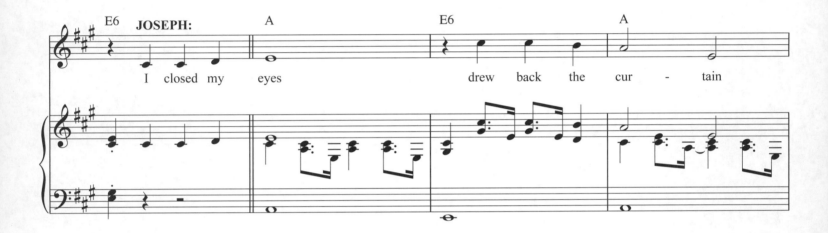

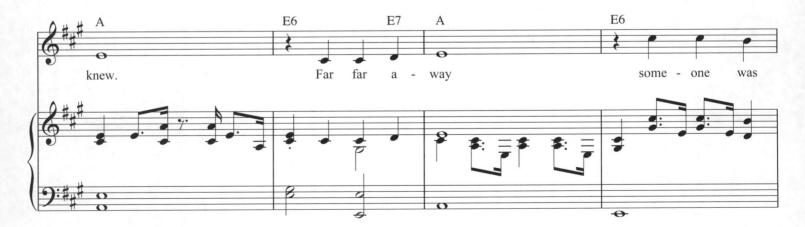

weep - ing, but the world was sleep - ing,

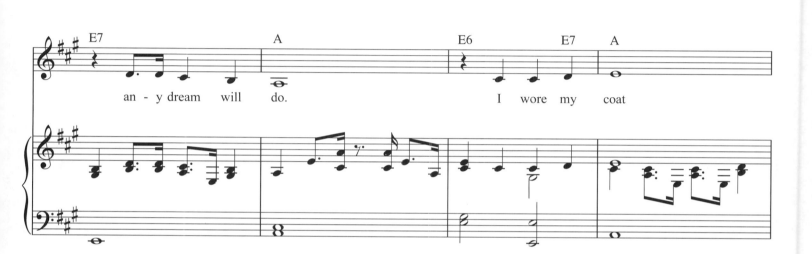

an - y dream will do. I wore my coat

with gold - en lin - ing, bright col - ours

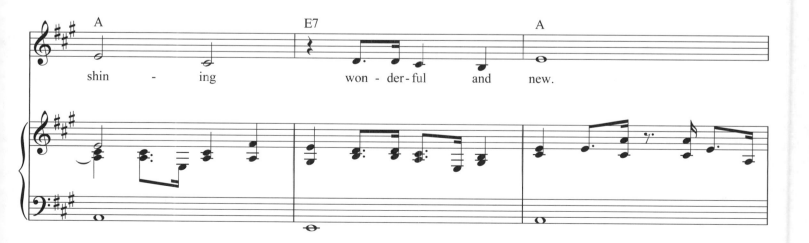

shin - ing won - der-ful and new.

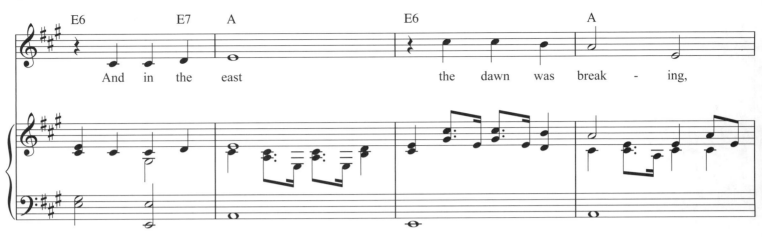

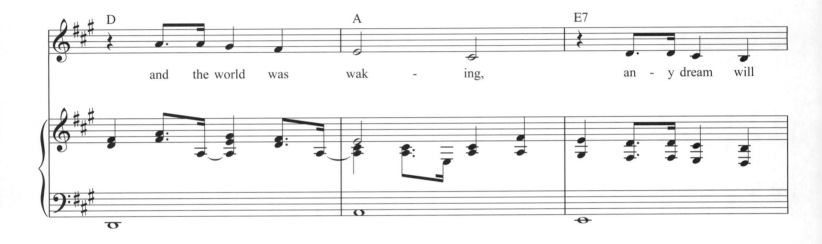

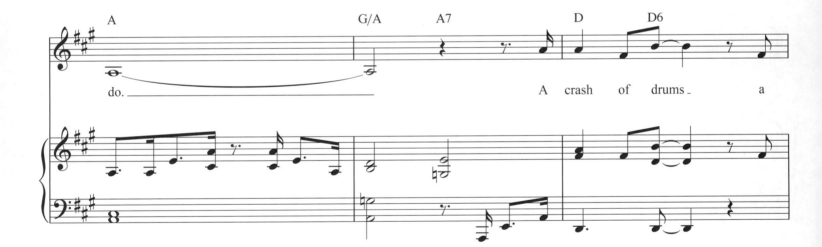

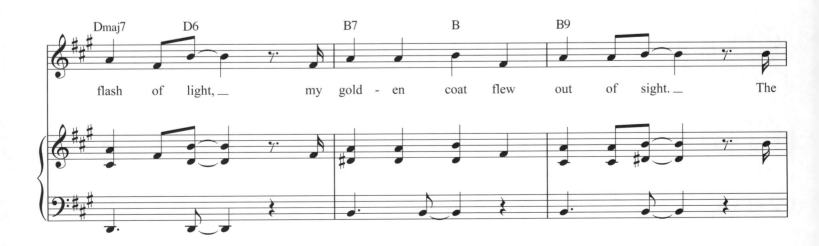

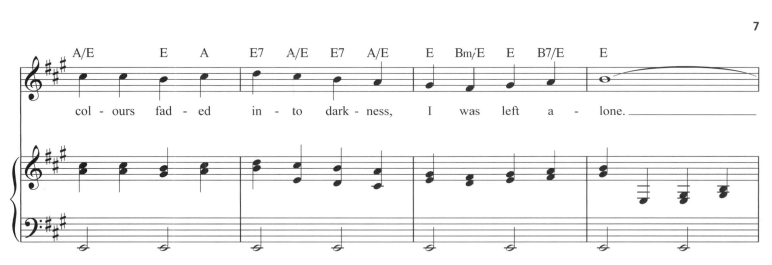

col - ours fad - ed in - to dark - ness, I was left a - lone.

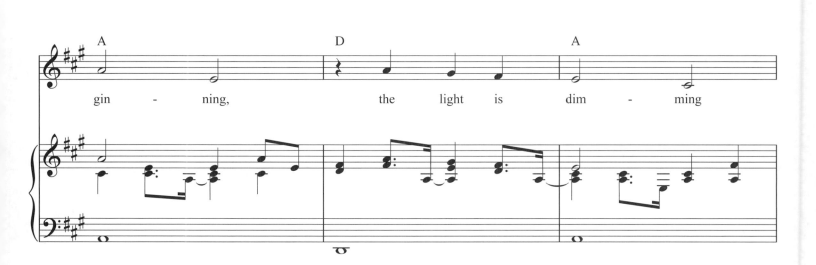

\_\_\_\_ May I re - turn, to the be -

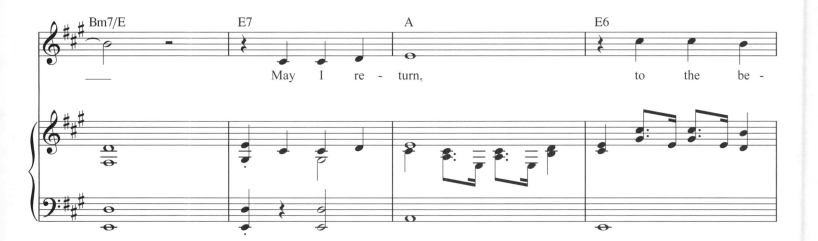

gin - ning, the light is dim - ming

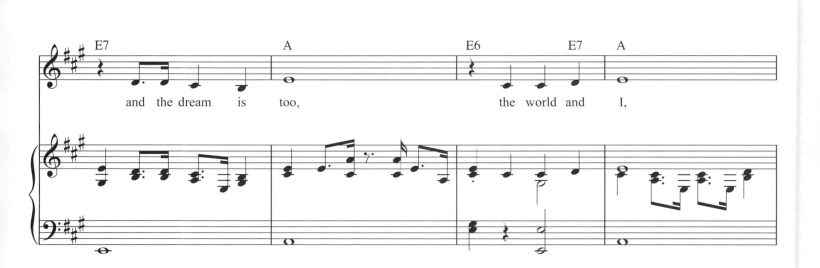

and the dream is too, the world and I,

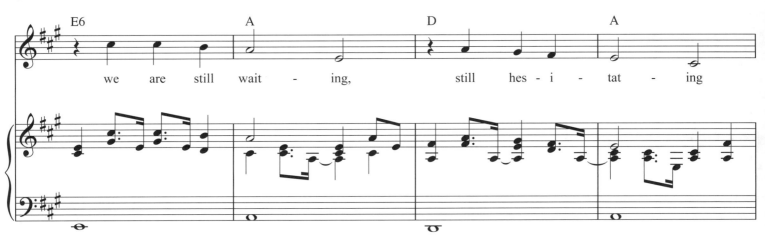

we are still wait - ing, still hes - i - tat - ing

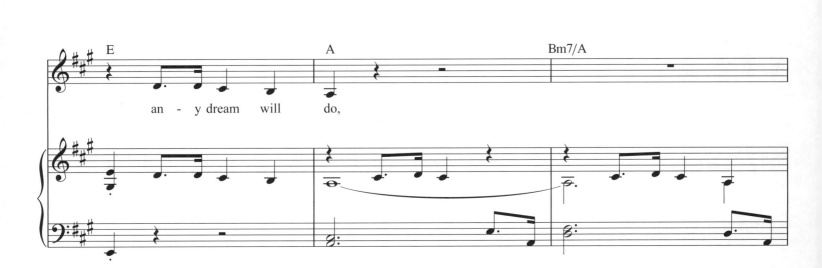

an - y dream will do,

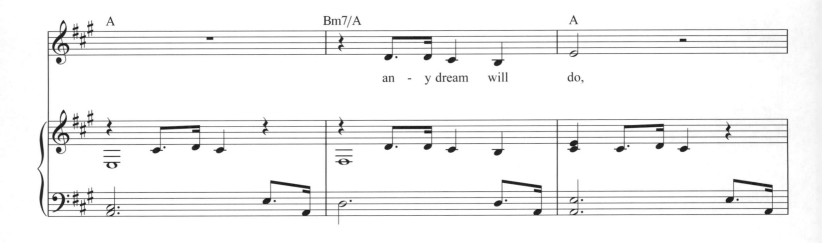

an - y dream will do,

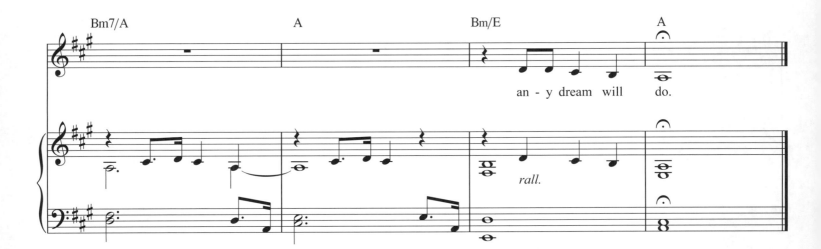

an - y dream will do.

rall.

# ANYTHING GOES

## from ANYTHING GOES

Words and Music by
COLE PORTER

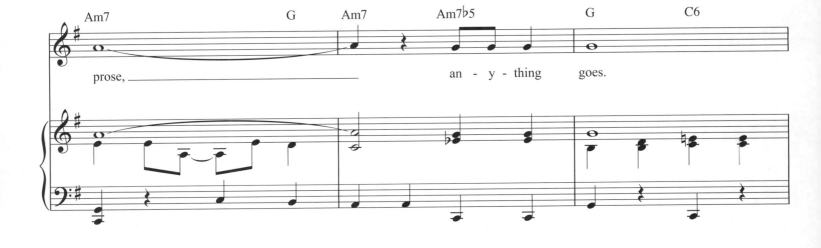

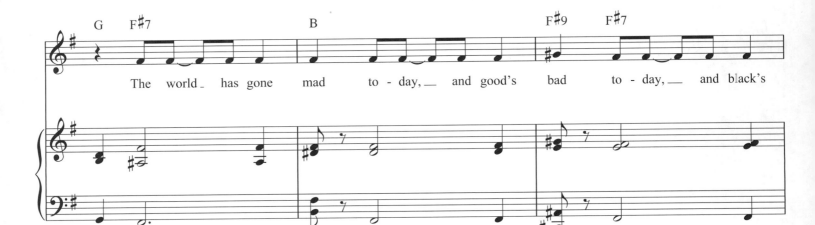

prize to - day ___ are just sil - ly gi - go - los. ___ So,

though I'm not a great ro - manc - er, I know that {you're / I'm} bound to an -

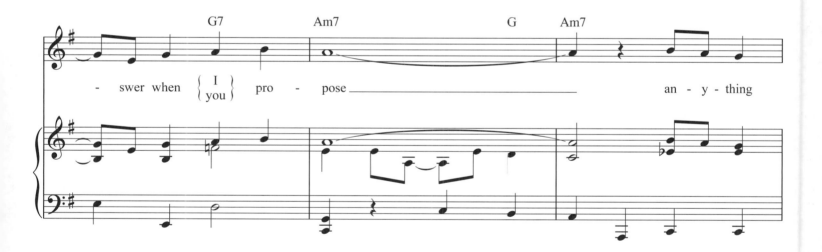

- swer when {I / you} pro - pose ___ an - y - thing

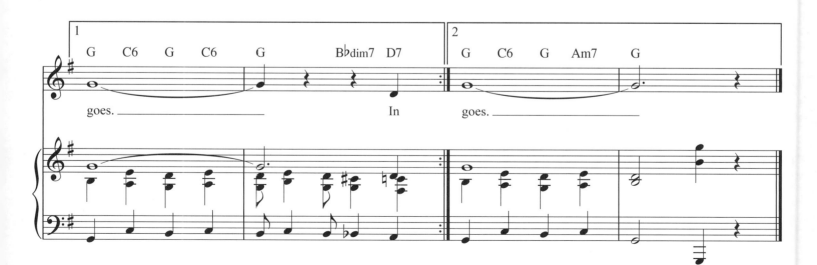

goes. ___ In goes. ___

# AS LONG AS HE NEEDS ME

## from the Broadway Musical OLIVER!

Words and Music by
LIONEL BART

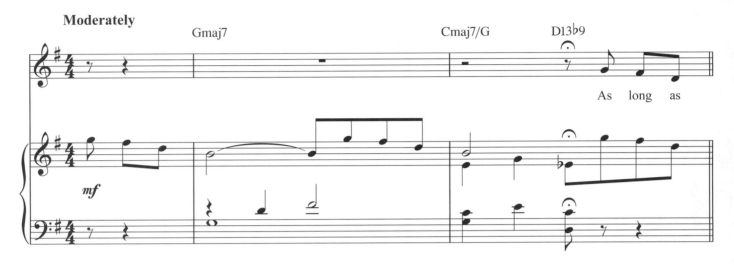

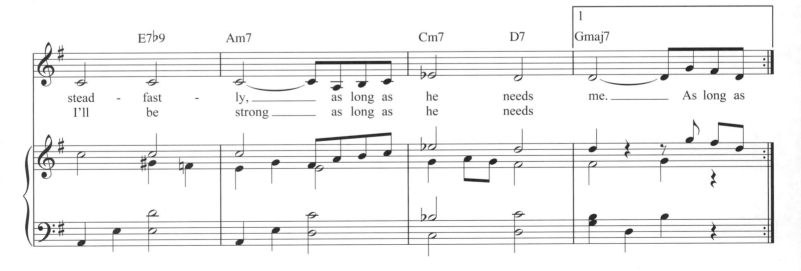

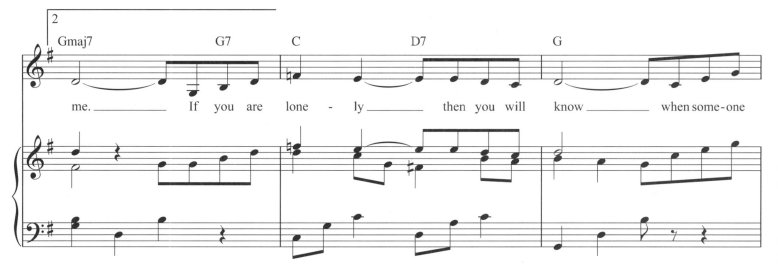

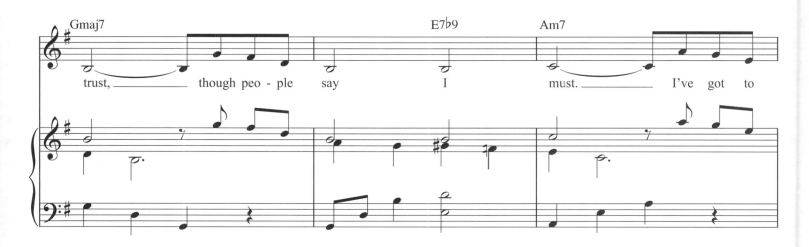

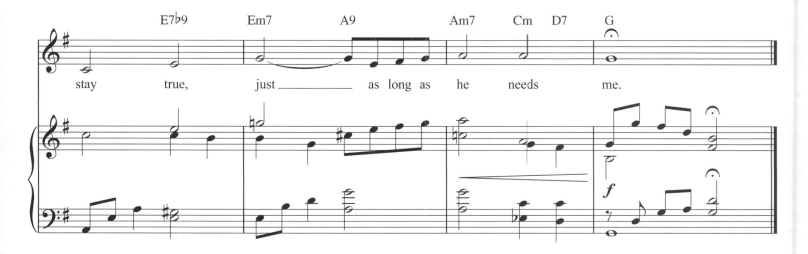

# BEAUTY AND THE BEAST

## from BEAUTY AND THE BEAST: THE BROADWAY MUSICAL

Music by ALAN MENKEN
Lyrics by HOWARD ASHMAN

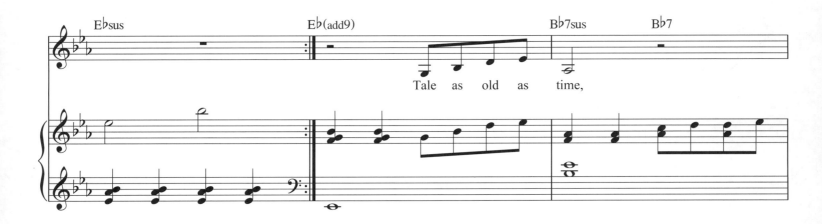

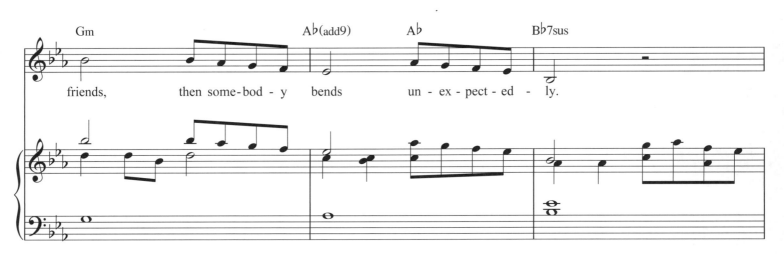

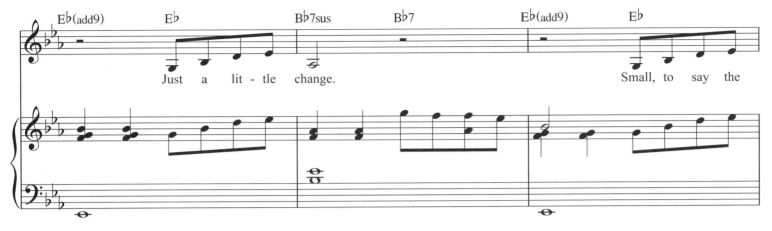

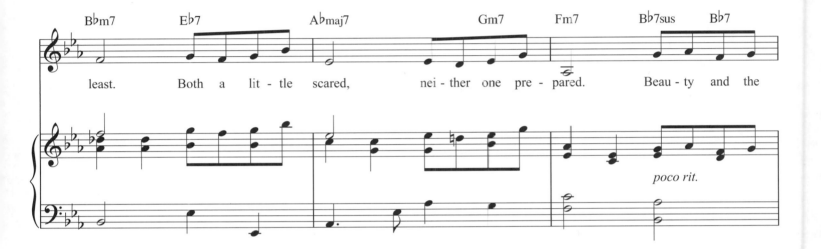

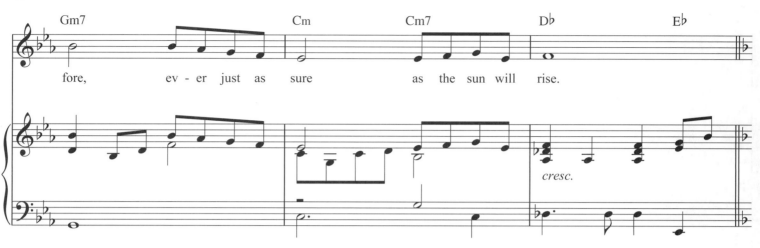

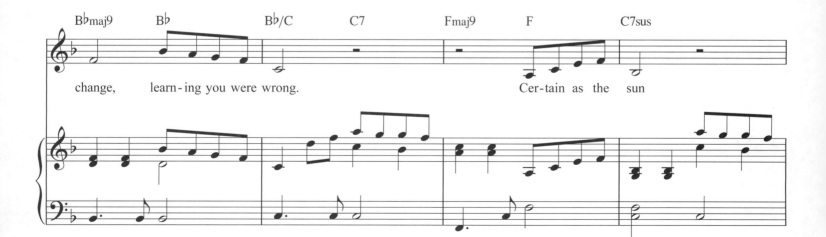

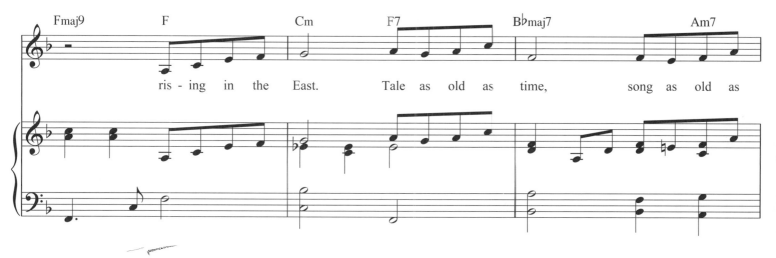

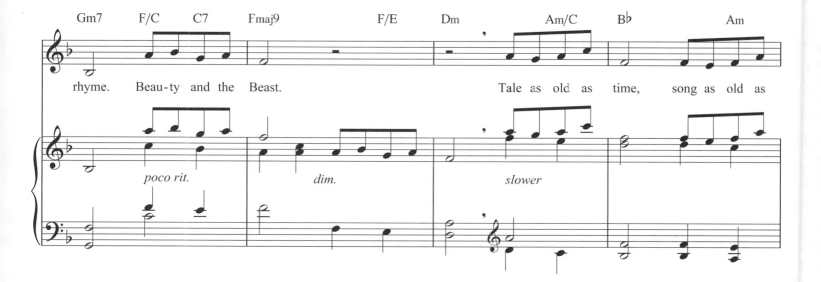

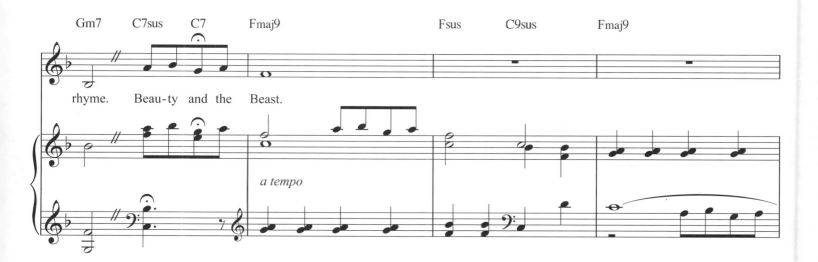

# BROADWAY BABY

## from FOLLIES

Music and Lyrics by
STEPHEN SONDHEIM

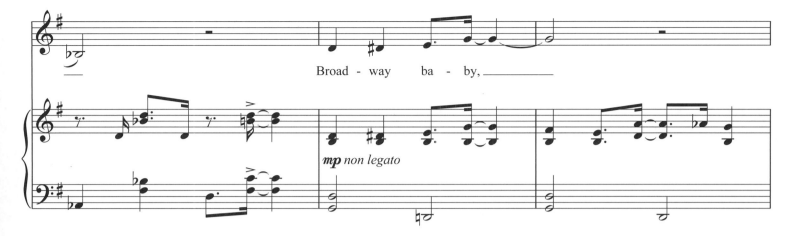

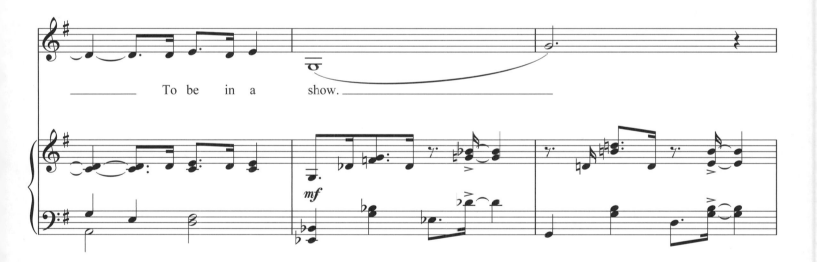

20

-kl-ing lights, A spark To pierce the dark From Bat - t'ry Park

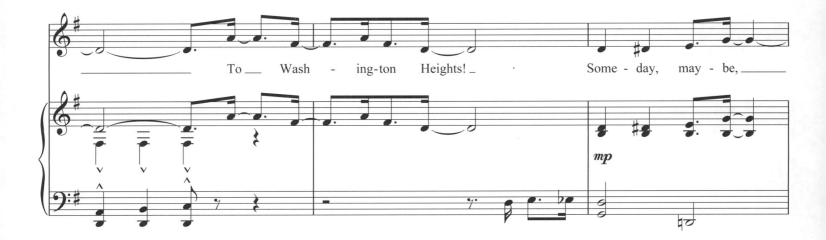

To Wash - ing-ton Heights! Some - day, may - be,

All my dreams will be re - paid.

Hell, I'd ev - en play the maid To be in a show.

Dream-ing of the great day when _____ I'll be in a

show.

Broad-way ba - by, _____ Mak - ing rounds all af - ter - noon,

mp non legato

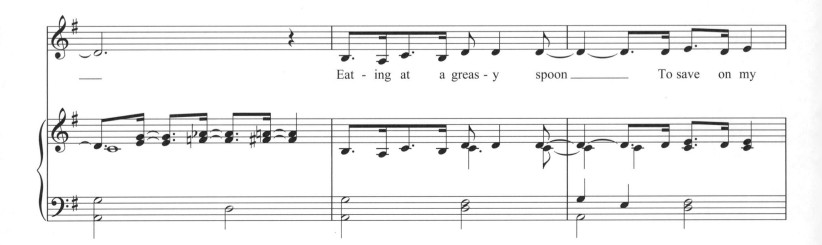

Eat - ing at a greas-y spoon _____ To save on my

24

# CAN'T HELP LOVIN' DAT MAN

## from SHOW BOAT

Lyrics by OSCAR HAMMERSTEIN II
Music by JEROME KERN

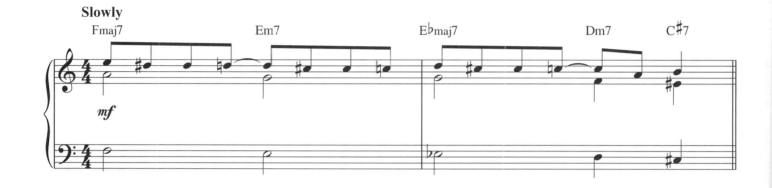

Fish got to swim and birds got to fly, ___ I got to love ___ one
Tell me he's la - zy, tell me he's slow, ___ tell me I'm cra - zy,

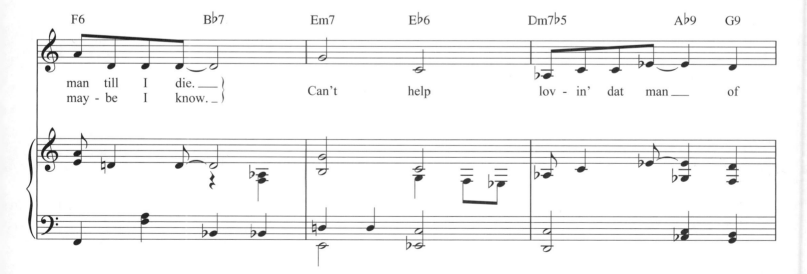

man till I die. ___ }
may - be I know. ___ } Can't help lov - in' dat man ___ of

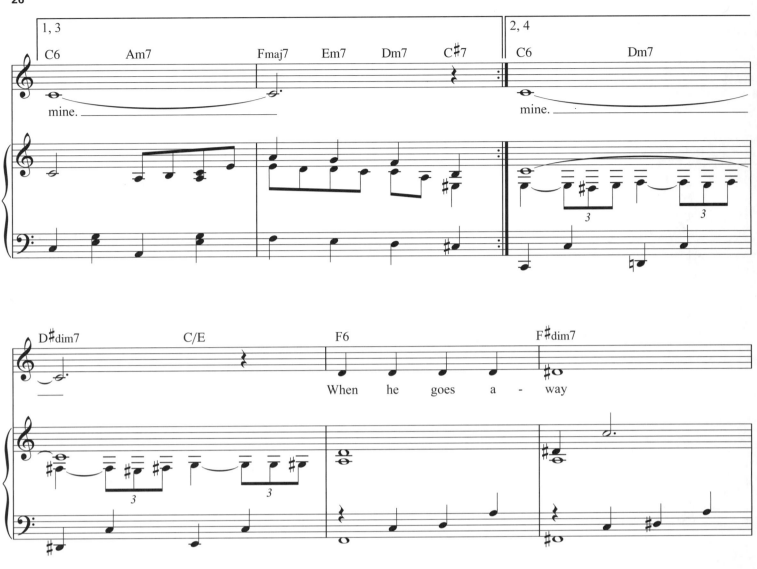

**1, 3** C6 Am7 Fmaj7 Em7 Dm7 C♯7 | **2, 4** C6 Dm7

mine. _____ mine. _____

D♯dim7 C/E F6 F♯dim7

When he goes a - way

C/G D7/A C/G

dat's a rain - y day, and when he comes

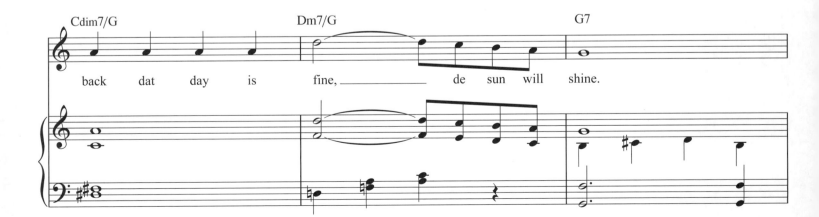

Cdim7/G Dm7/G G7

back dat day is fine, _____ de sun will shine.

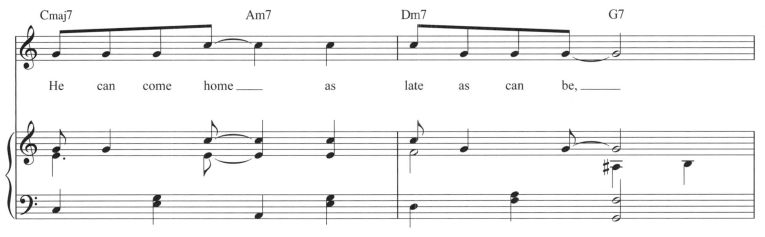

He can come home ___ as late as can be, ___

home wid - out him ___ ain't no home to me. ___

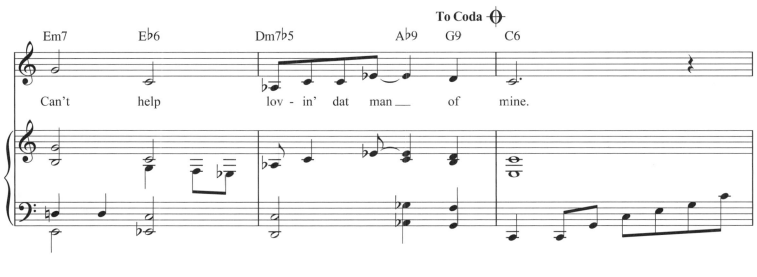

**To Coda** ⊕

Can't help lov - in' dat man ___ of mine.

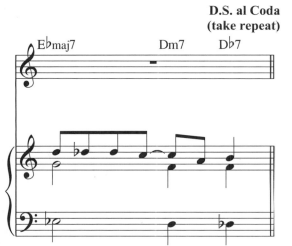

**D.S. al Coda**
**(take repeat)**

**CODA** ⊕

mine. ___

# CABARET
## from the Musical CABARET

Words by FRED EBB
Music by JOHN KANDER

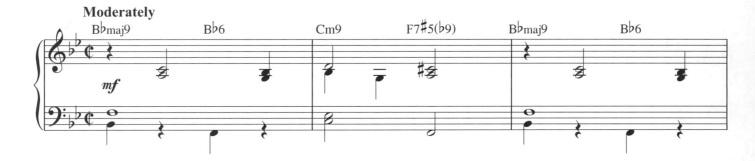

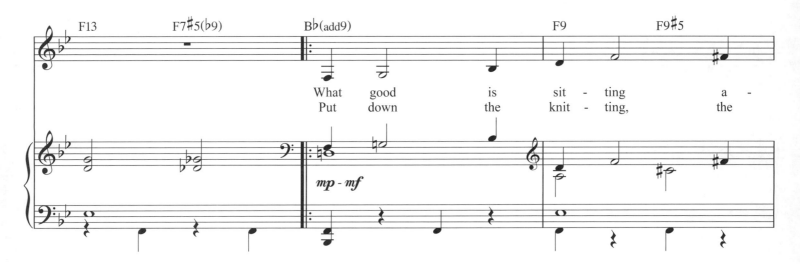

What good is sit - ting a -
Put down the knit - ting, the

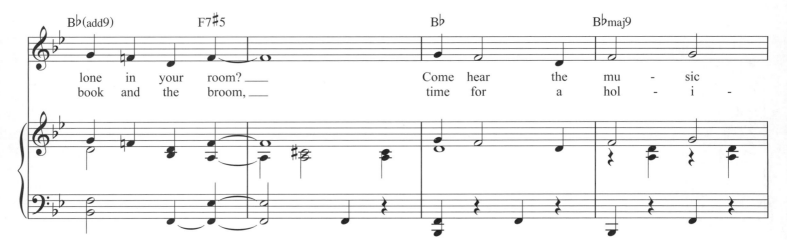

lone in your room? ___ Come hear the mu - sic
book and the broom, ___ time for a hol - i -

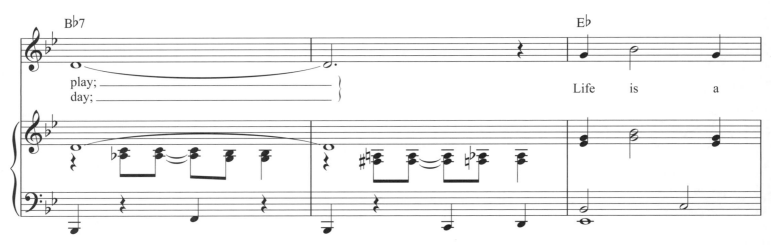

play; ___
day; ___

Life is a

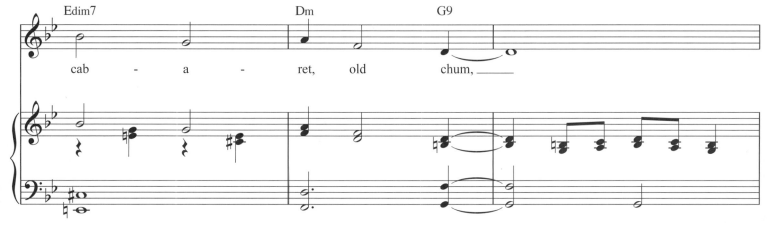

cab - a - ret, old chum, _____

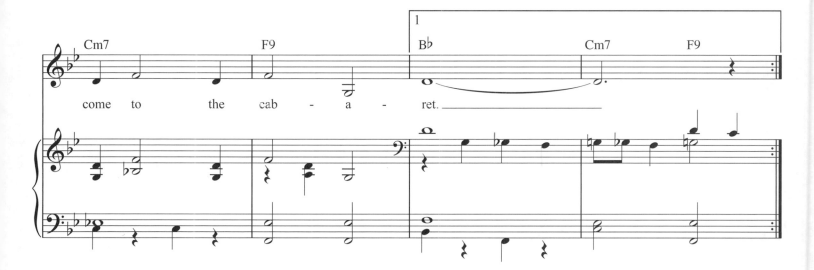

come to the cab - a - ret. _____

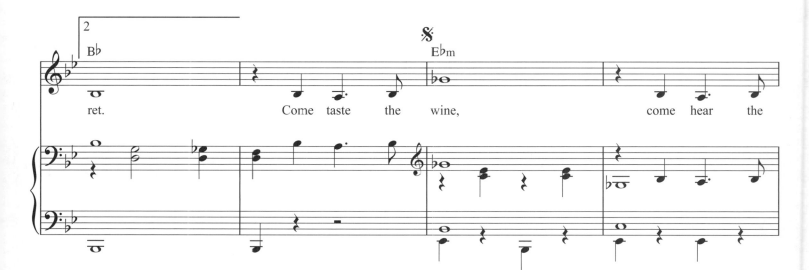

ret. Come taste the wine, come hear the

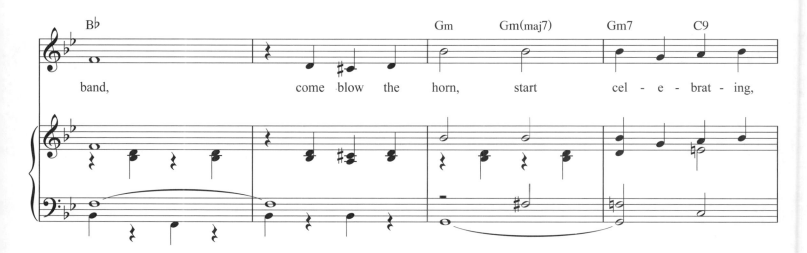

band, come blow the horn, start cel - e - brat - ing,

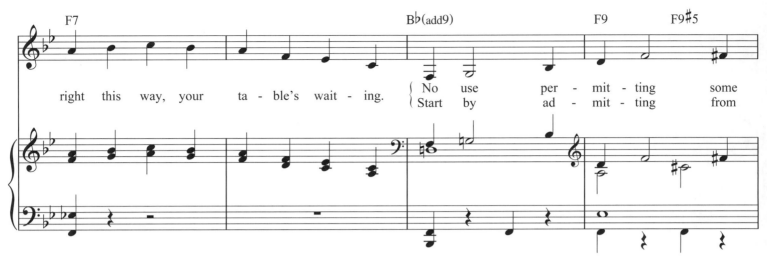

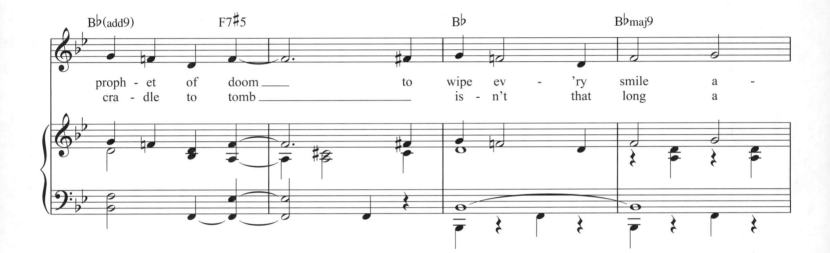

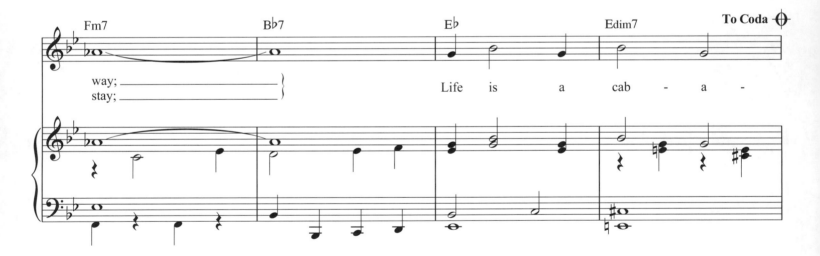

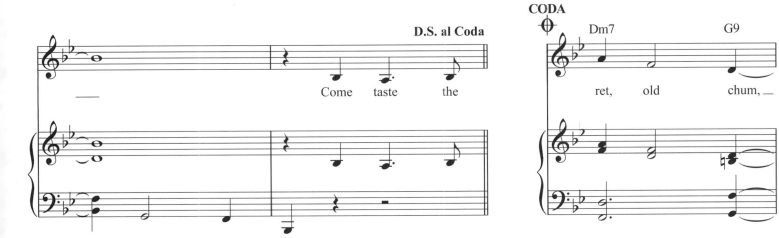

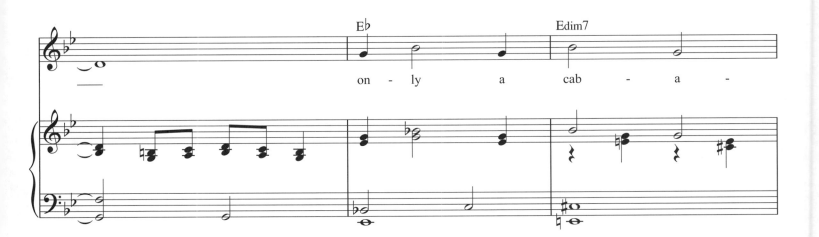

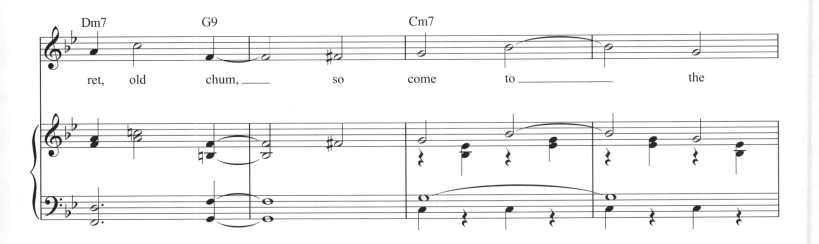

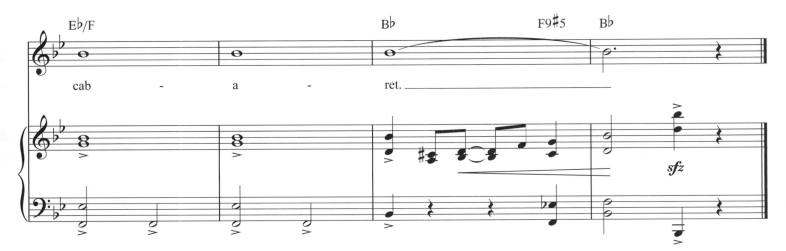

# COMEDY TONIGHT

## from A FUNNY THING HAPPENED ON THE WAY TO THE FORUM

Music and Lyrics by
STEPHEN SONDHEIM

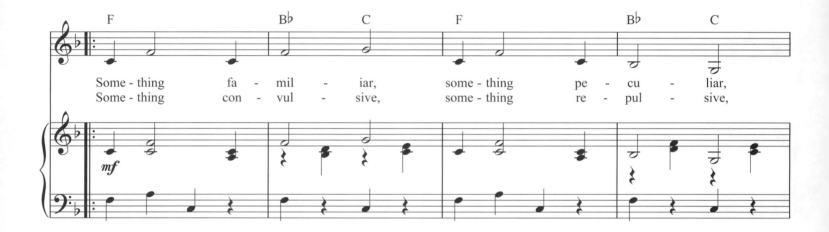

Some - thing fa - mil - iar, some - thing pe - cu - liar,
Some - thing con - vul - sive, some - thing re - pul - sive,

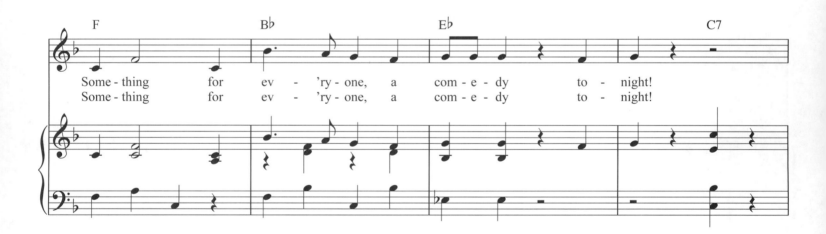

Some - thing for ev - 'ry - one, a com - e - dy to - night!
Some - thing for ev - 'ry - one, a com - e - dy to - night!

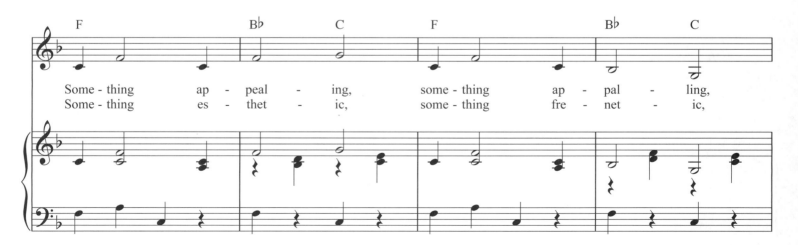

Some - thing ap - peal - ing, some - thing ap - pal - ling,
Some - thing es - thet - ic, some - thing fre - net - ic,

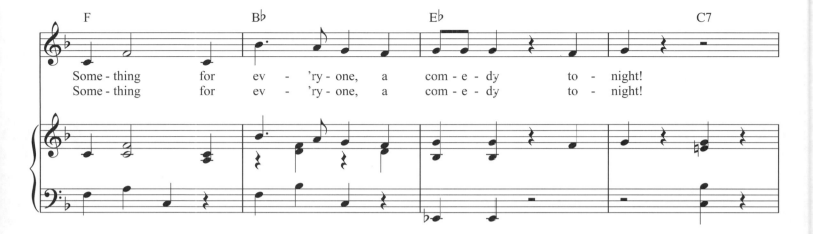

Some - thing for ev - 'ry - one, a com - e - dy to - night!
Some - thing for ev - 'ry - one, a com - e - dy to - night!

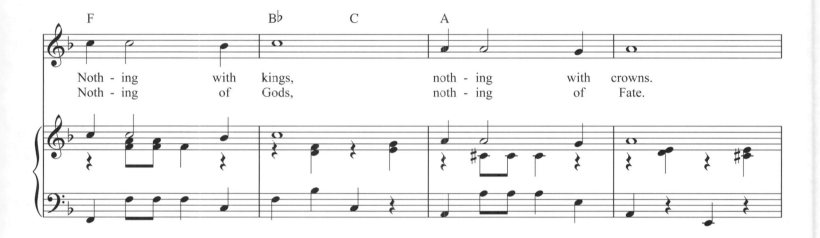

Noth - ing with kings, noth - ing with crowns.
Noth - ing of Gods, noth - ing of Fate.

Bring on the lov - ers, li - ars and clowns! _____
Weigh - ty af - fairs will just have to wait. _____

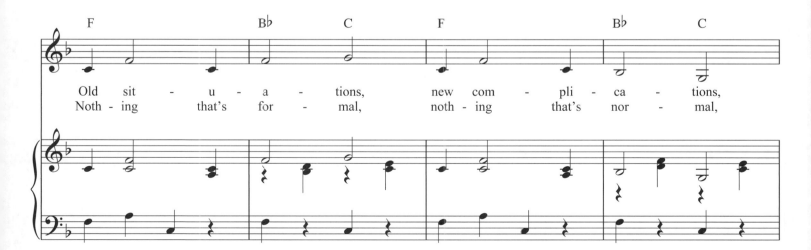

Old sit - u - a - tions, new com - pli - ca - tions,
Noth - ing that's for - mal, noth - ing that's nor - mal,

# EDELWEISS
## from THE SOUND OF MUSIC

Lyrics by OSCAR HAMMERSTEIN II
Music by RICHARD RODGERS

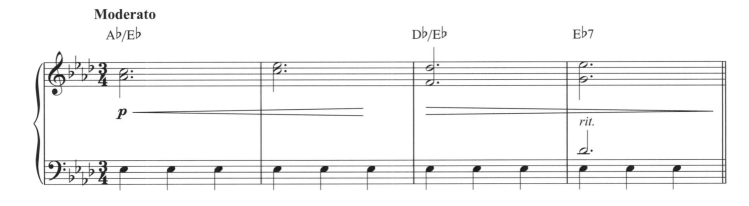

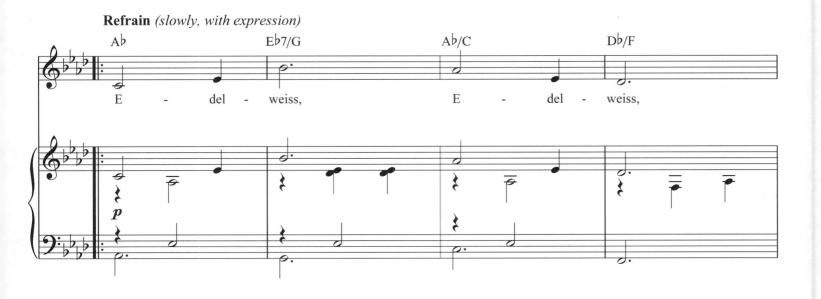

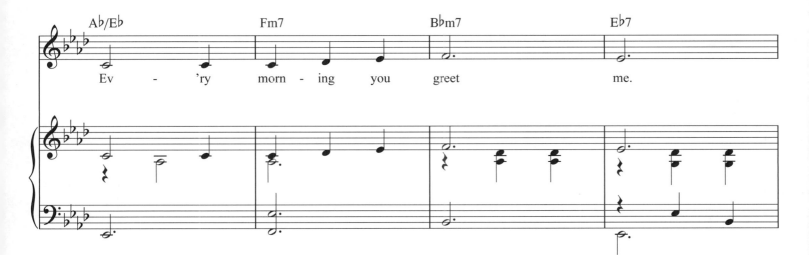

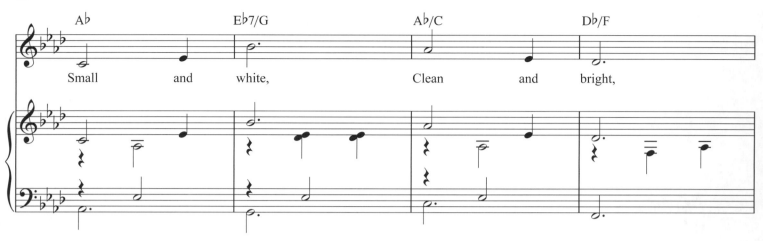

Small and white, Clean and bright,

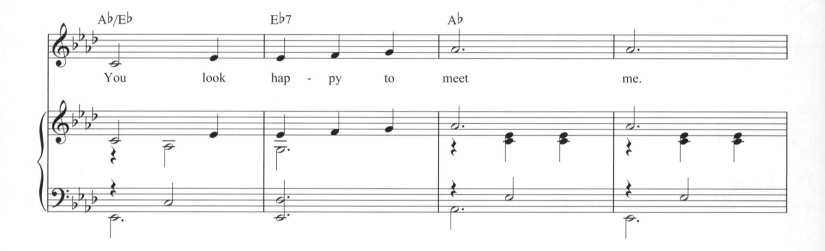

You look hap-py to meet me.

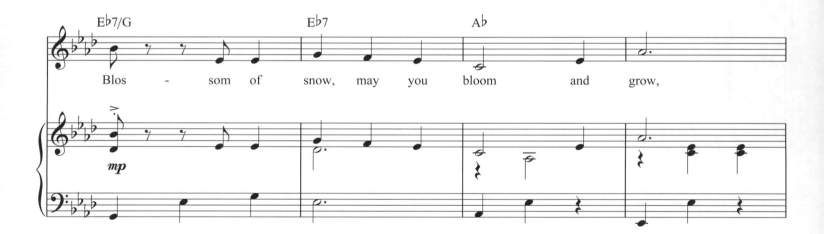

Blos - som of snow, may you bloom and grow,

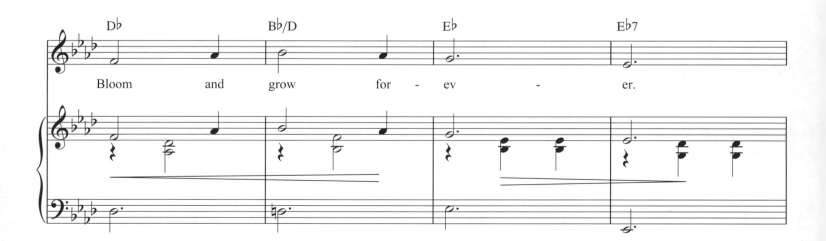

Bloom and grow for - ev - er.

# DON'T CRY FOR ME ARGENTINA

## from EVITA

Words by TIM RICE
Music by ANDREW LLOYD WEBBER

Slowly

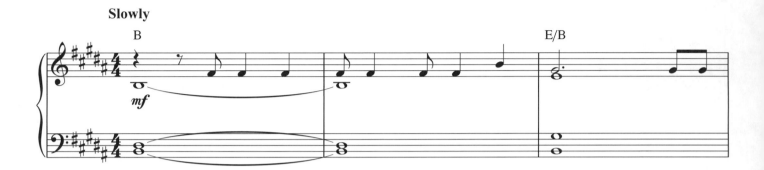

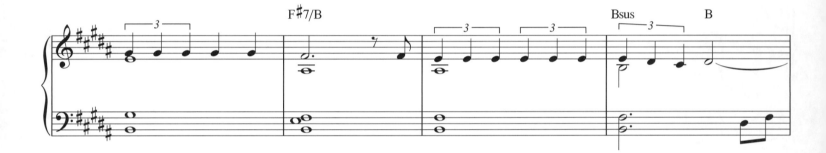

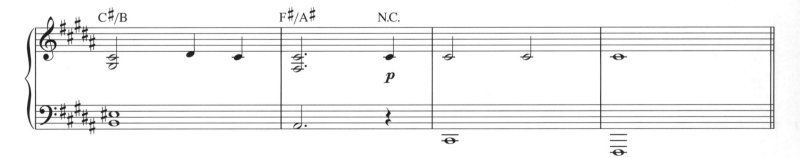

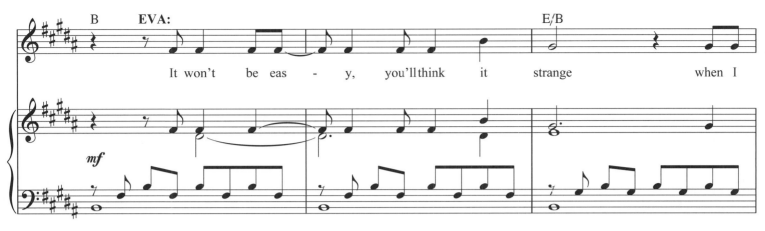

It won't be eas - y, you'll think it strange when I

try to ex-plain how I feel, that I still need your love af - ter

all that I've done. _____ You won't be - lieve me.

All you will see is a girl you once knew, al - though she's dressed up to the

40

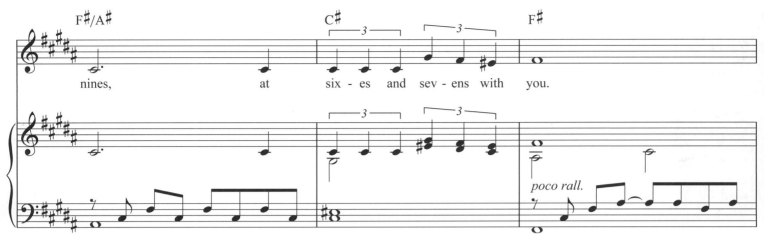

nines, at six - es and sev - ens with you.

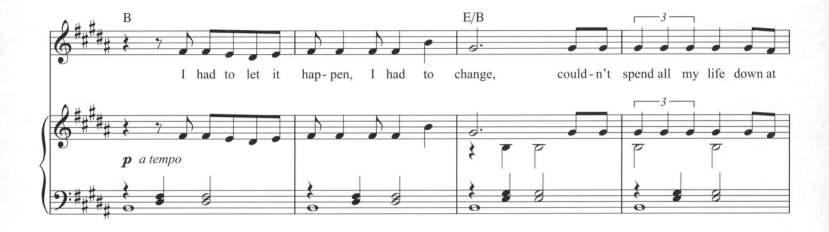

I had to let it hap - pen, I had to change, could-n't spend all my life down at

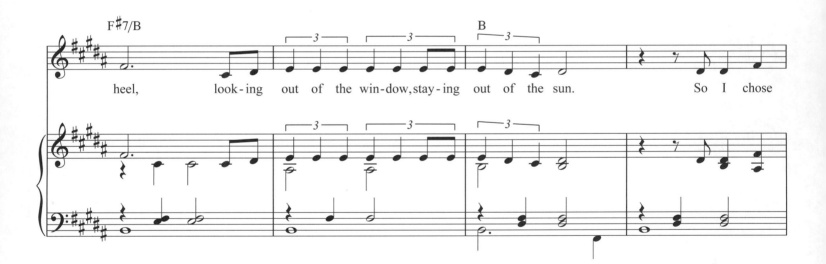

heel, look - ing out of the win-dow, stay-ing out of the sun. So I chose

free - dom, run-ning a - round try-ing ev - 'ry-thing new, but noth-ing im - pressed me at all, _

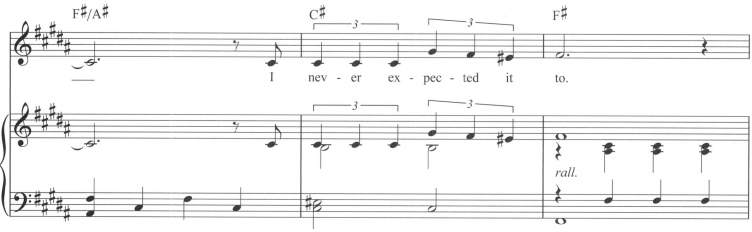

I nev-er ex-pec-ted it to.

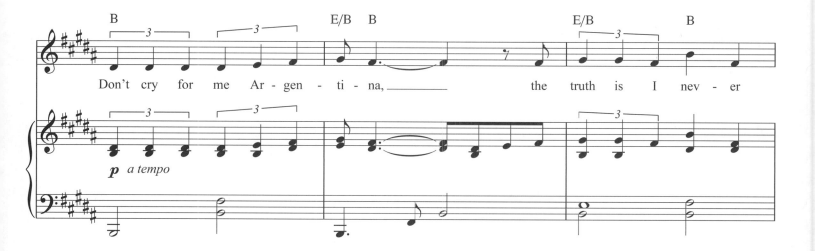

Don't cry for me Ar-gen-ti-na,_____ the truth is I nev-er

left you. All through my wild days,_____ my mad ex-is-tence,_____ I kept my

prom-ise, don't keep your dis-tance._____

And as for for - tune and as for fame, I

nev - er in - vit - ed them in, though it seemed to the world __ they were

all I de - sired. They are il - lu - sions, they're

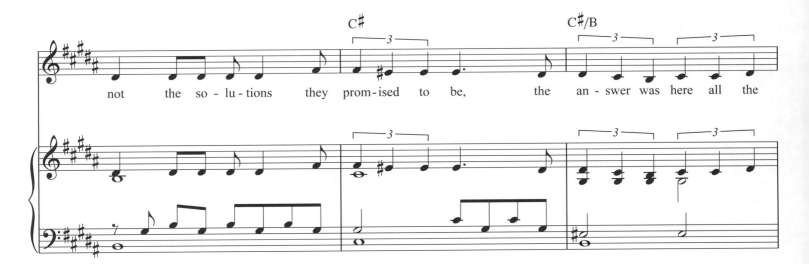

not the so - lu - tions they prom - ised to be, the an - swer was here all the

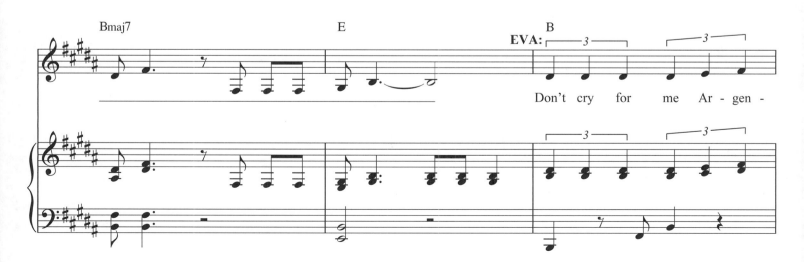

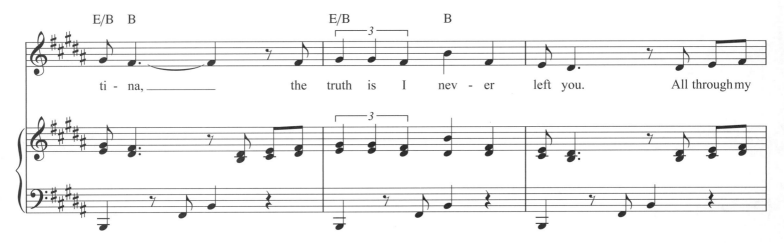

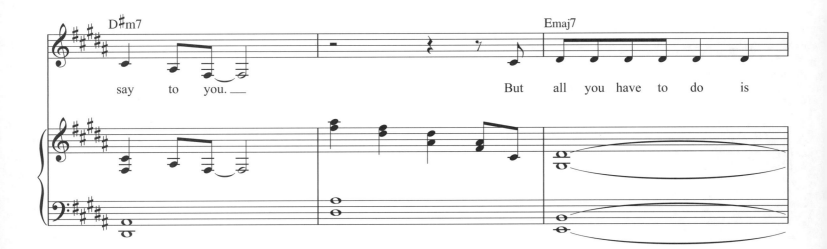

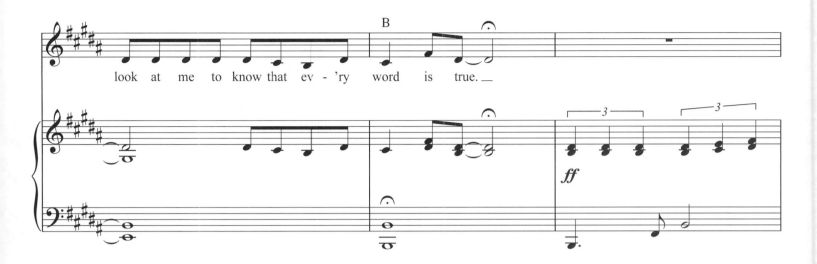

look at me to know that ev - 'ry word is true. __

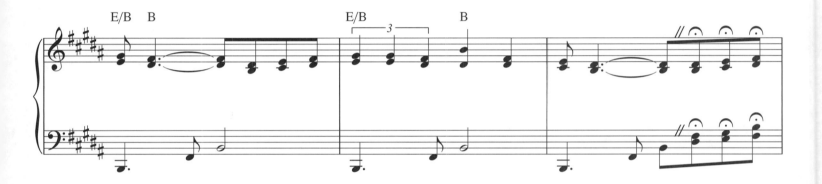

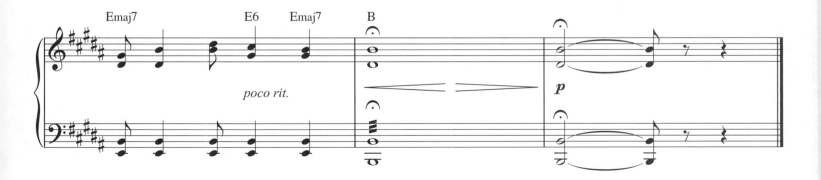

# EVERYTHING'S COMING UP ROSES

## from GYPSY

Lyrics by STEPHEN SONDHEIM
Music by JULE STYNE

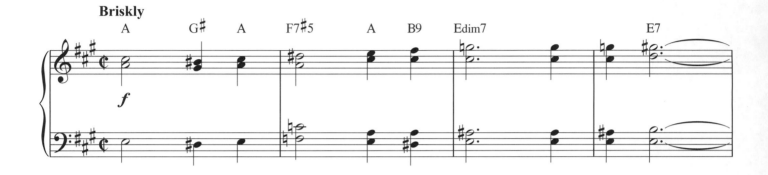

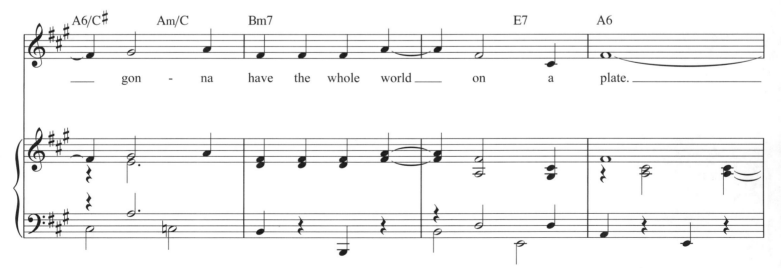

47

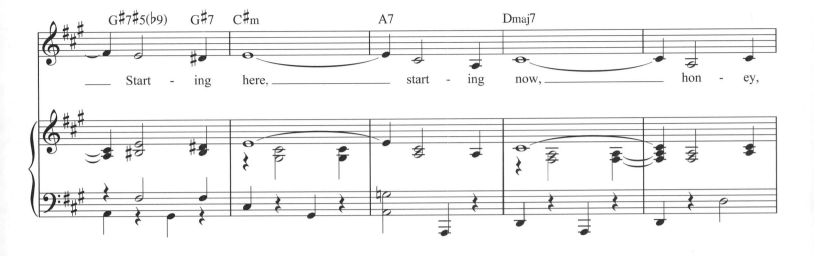

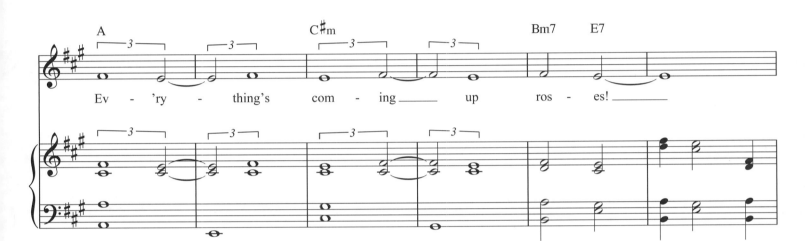

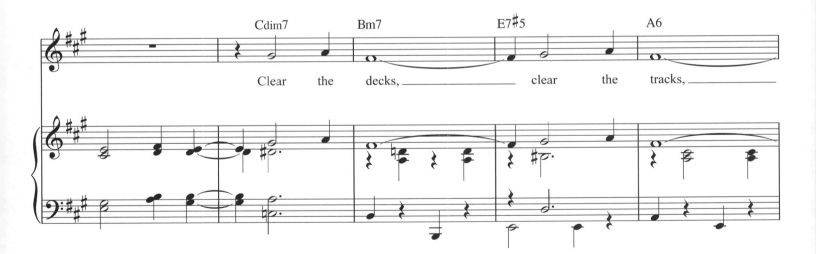

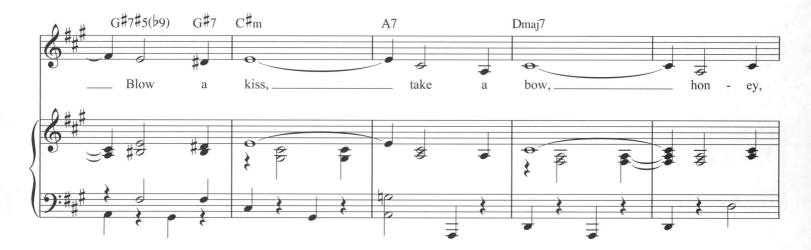

Blow a kiss, _____ take a bow, _____ hon - ey,

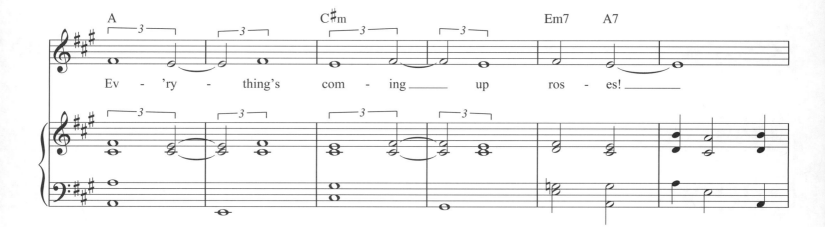

Ev - 'ry - thing's com - ing _____ up ros - es! _____

Now's our _____

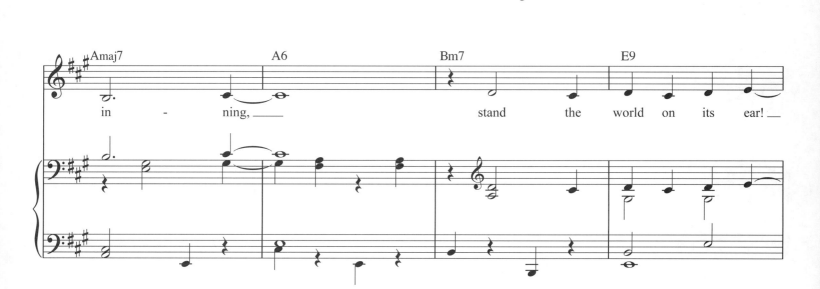

in - ning, _____ stand the world on its ear! __

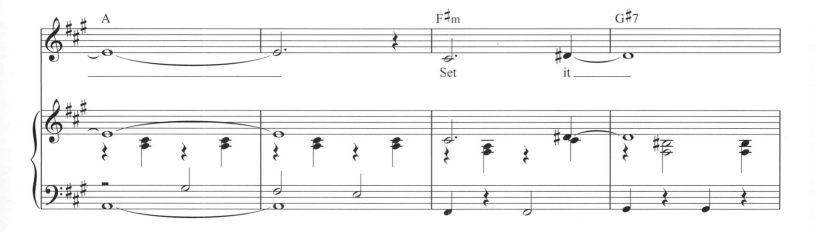

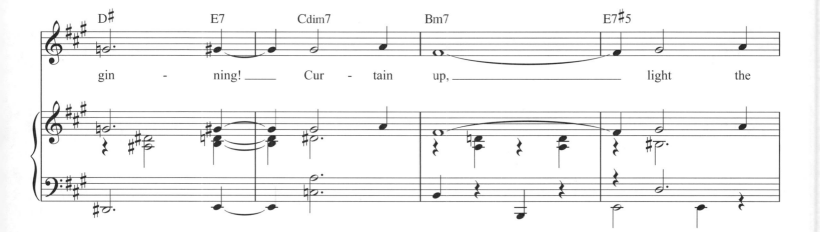

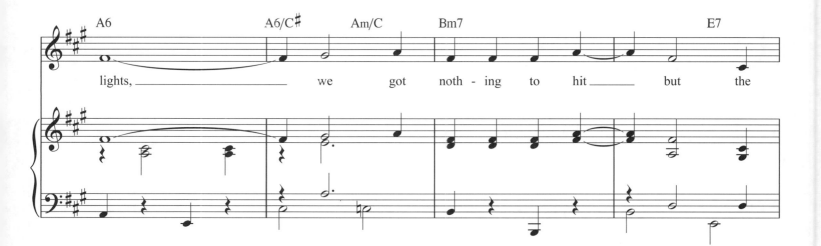

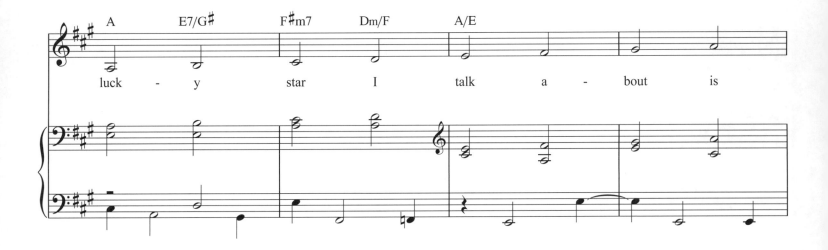

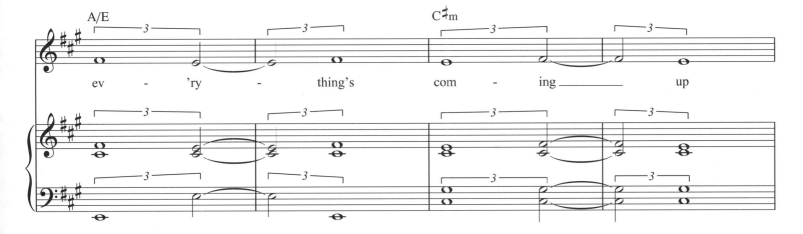

ev - 'ry - thing's com - ing _____ up

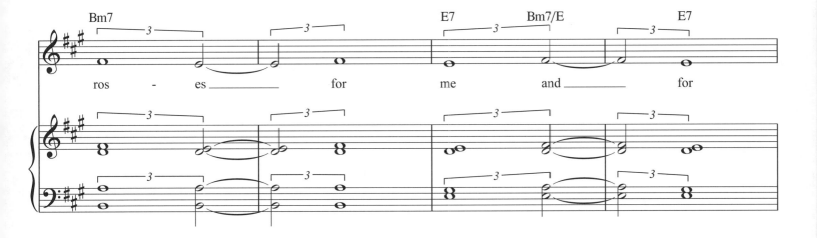

ros - es _____ for me and _____ for

you! _____ Things look

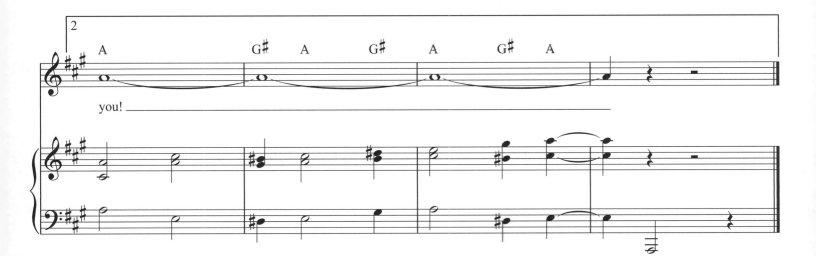

you! _____

# FOR GOOD
## from the Broadway Musical WICKED

Music and Lyrics by
STEPHEN SCHWARTZ

*Note: When performed as a solo, sing the top melody line throughout.*

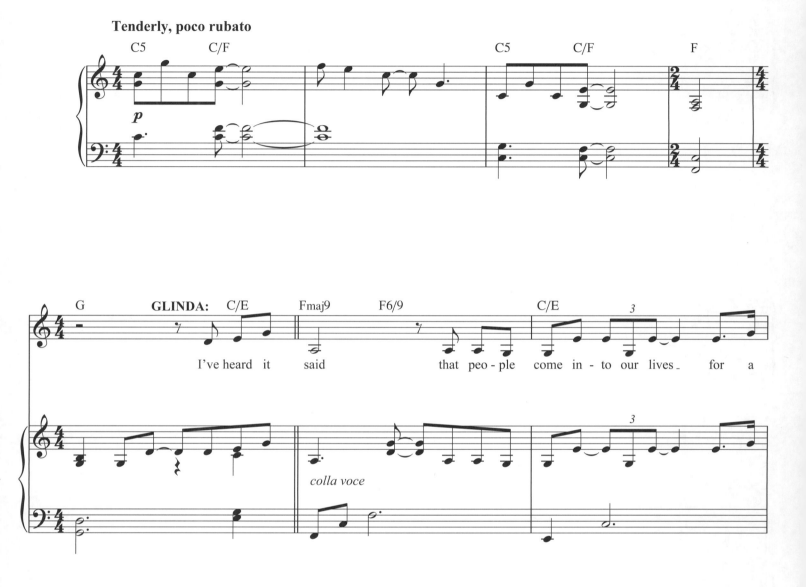

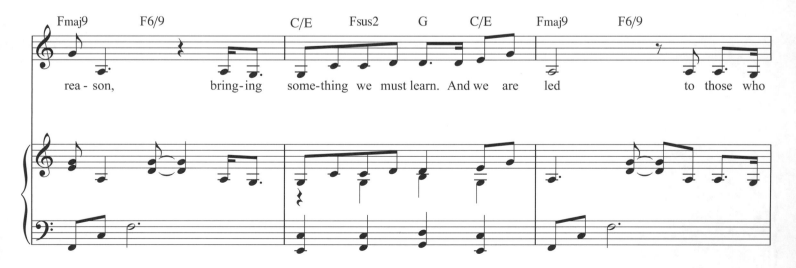

help us most to grow, __ if we let them, _____ and we help them in ___ re - turn.

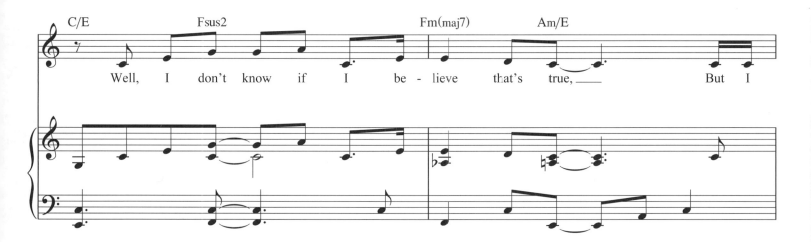

Well, I don't know if I be - lieve that's true, _____ But I

know I'm who I am __ to - day __ be - cause I knew you... _____ Like a

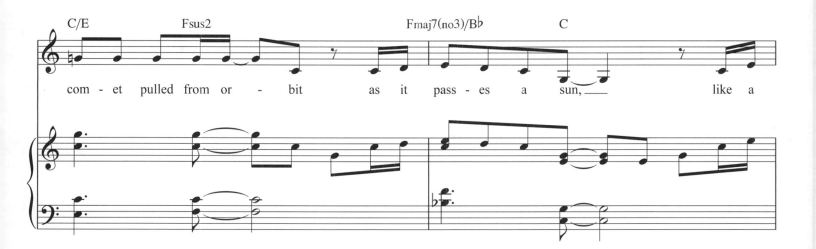

com - et pulled from or - bit as it pass - es a sun, _____ like a

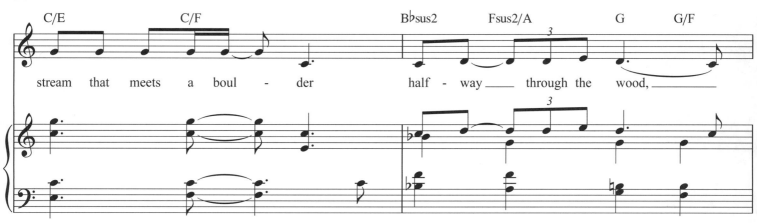

stream that meets a boul - der half - way ____ through the wood, ____

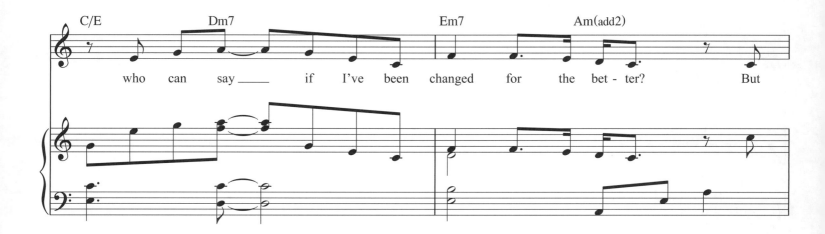

who can say ____ if I've been changed for the bet - ter? But

be - cause I knew you, I have been changed for

**A tempo, warmly**

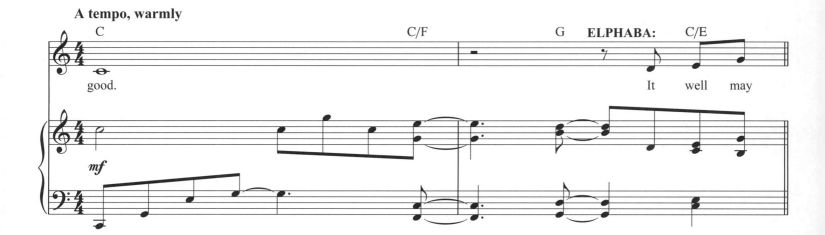

good. It well may

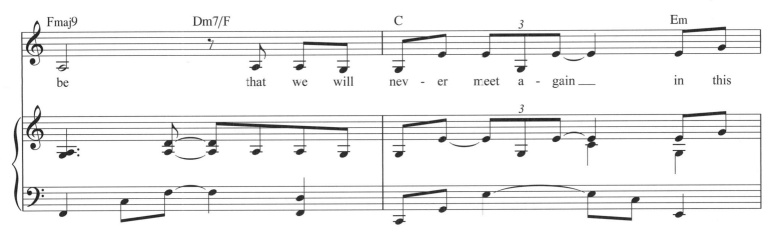

be that we will nev-er meet a-gain ___ in this

life-time, so ___ let me say be-fore ___ we part: ___ So much of ___

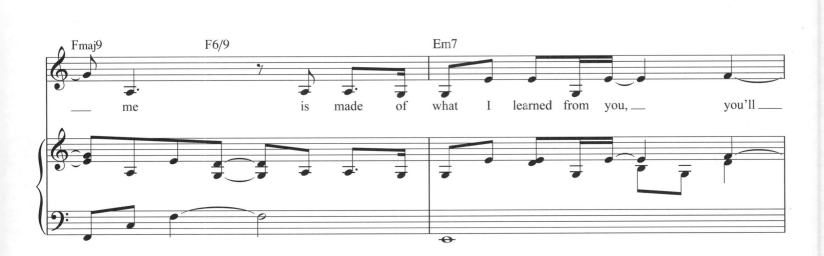

___ me is made of what I learned from you, ___ you'll ___

___ be with me ___ like a hand-print on my ___ heart.

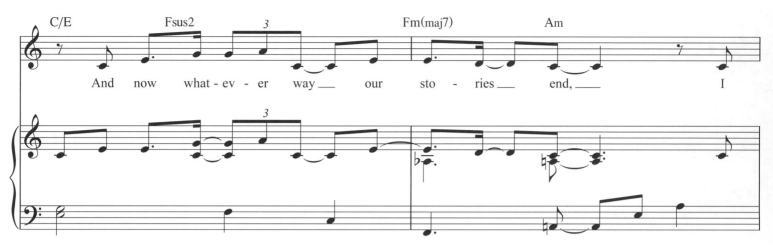

And now what-ev-er way ___ our sto - ries ___ end, ___ I

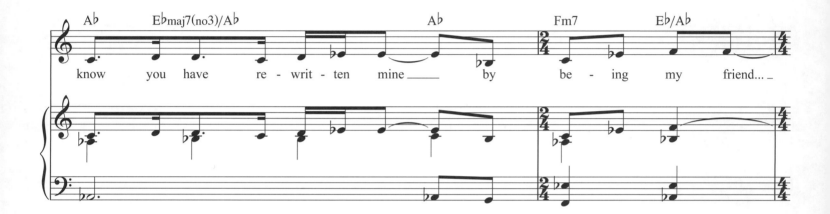

know you have re - writ - ten mine _____ by be - ing my friend... _

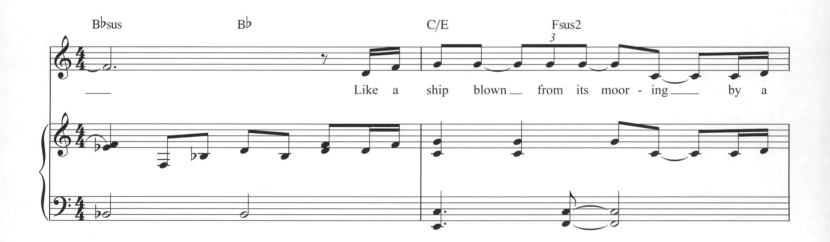

___ Like a ship blown ___ from its moor-ing _____ by a

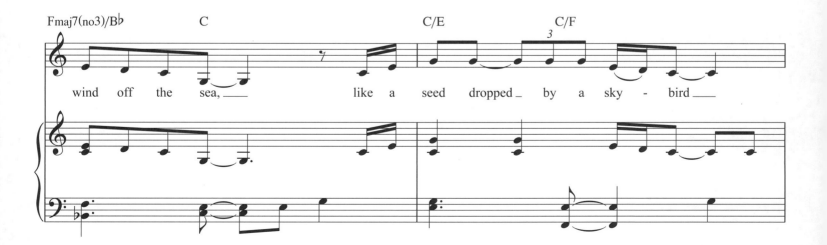

wind off the sea, ___ like a seed dropped _ by a sky - bird ___

57

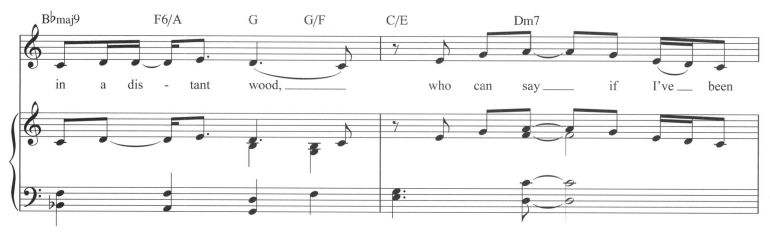

in a dis - tant wood, _____ who can say ____ if I've ____ been

changed for the bet - ter? But be - cause I knew you...

**Più mosso**

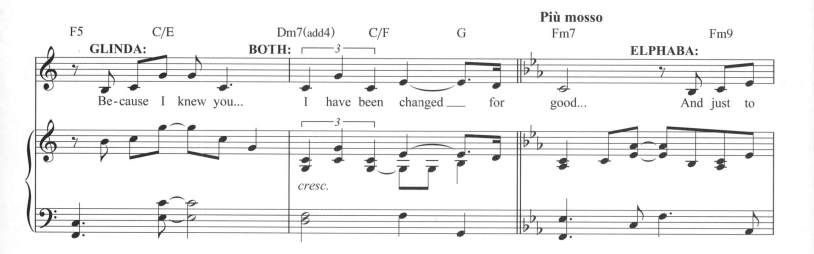

GLINDA: BOTH: Be-cause I knew you... I have been changed ____ for good... ELPHABA: And just to

clear the air, I ask for - give - ness for the things I've done ____ you

blame me ___ for. ___ But then, I guess_ we know there's

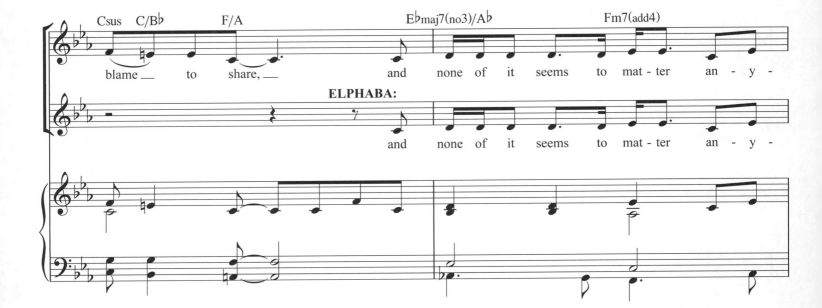

blame ___ to share, ___ and none of it seems to mat-ter an-y-

**ELPHABA:**

and none of it seems to mat-ter an-y-

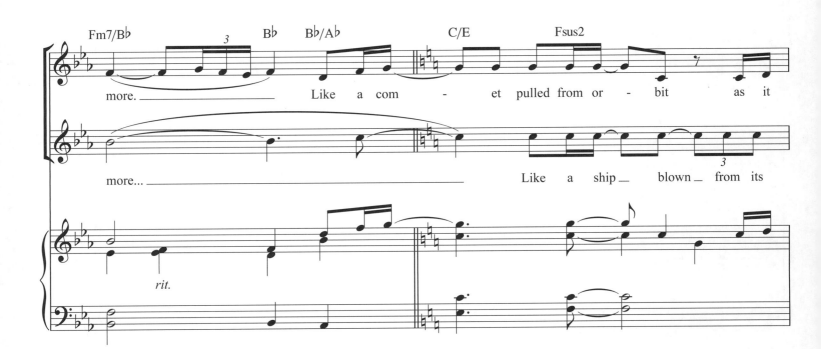

more. _____ Like a com - et pulled from or-bit as it

more... _____ Like a ship_ blown_ from its

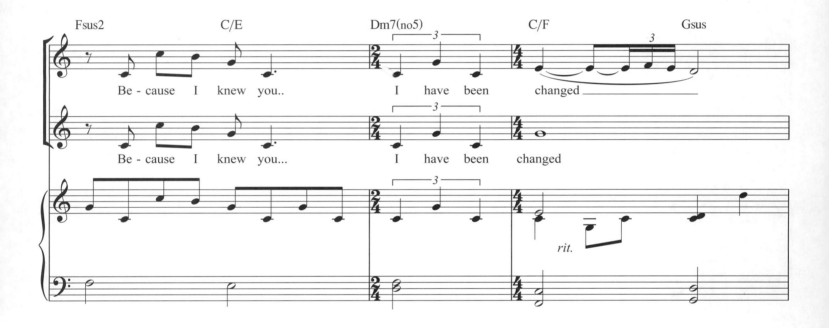

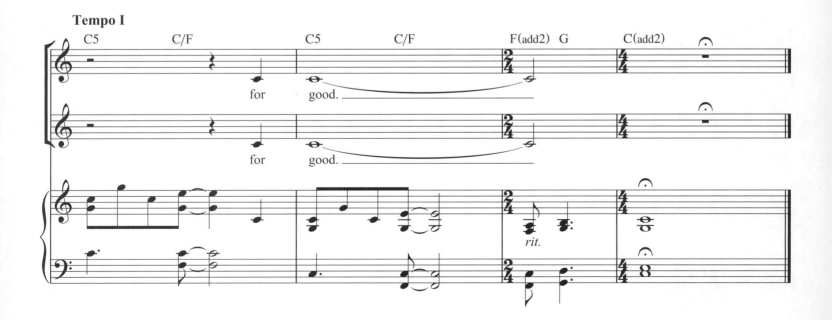

# I GOT THE SUN IN THE MORNING

### from the Stage Production ANNIE GET YOUR GUN

Words and Music by
IRVING BERLIN

**Light bounce**

Tak - ing stock __ of what I have __ and what I have - n't, _____ what do I find? __ The things I've got will keep me sat - is - fied. _____

63

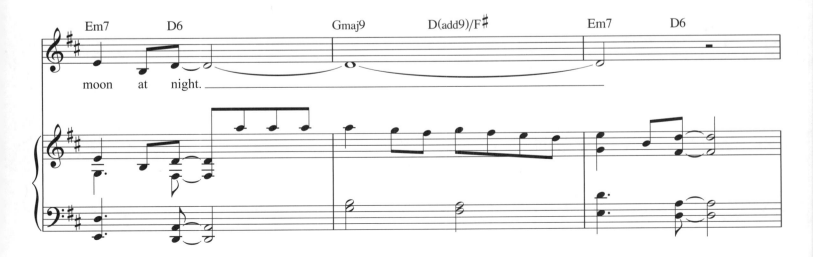

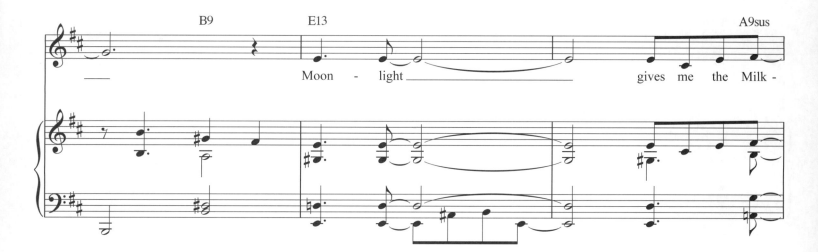

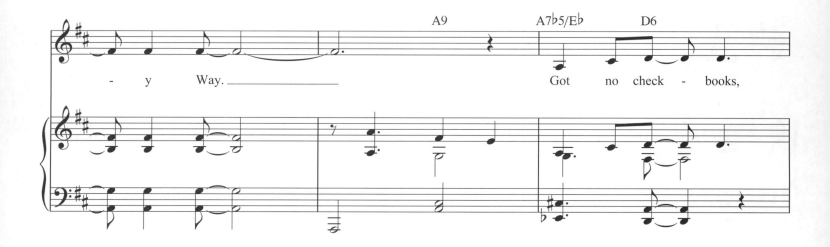

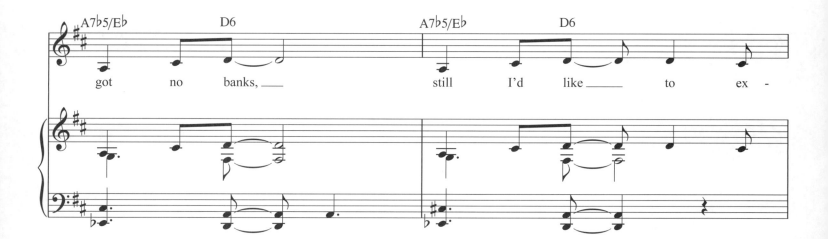

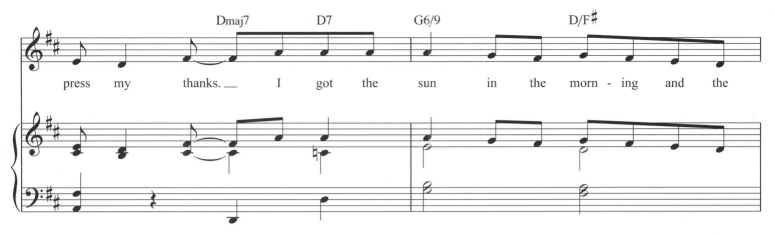

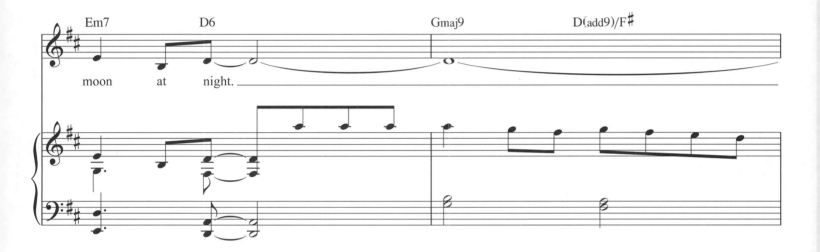

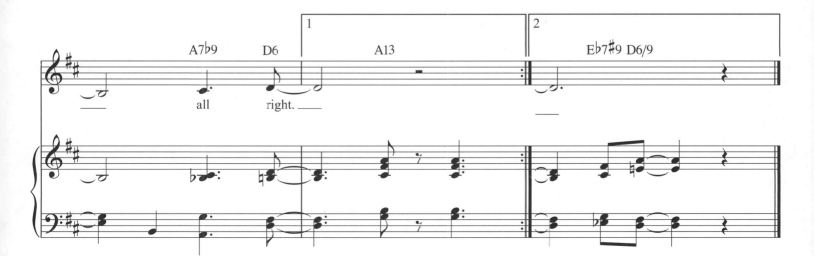

# GETTING TO KNOW YOU

## from THE KING AND I

Lyrics by OSCAR HAMMERSTEIN II
Music by RICHARD RODGERS

Get-ting to know you, Put-ting it my way, but nice - ly

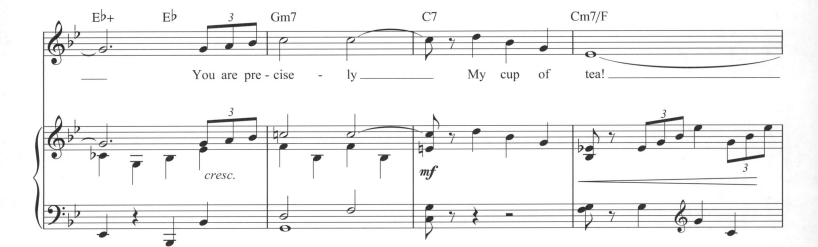

You are pre-cise - ly My cup of tea!

Get-ting to know you, get-ting to feel free and eas - y

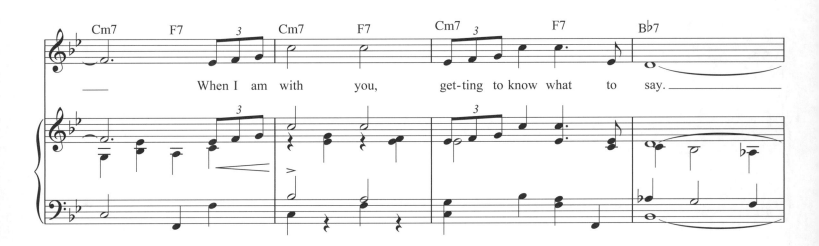

When I am with you, get-ting to know what to say.

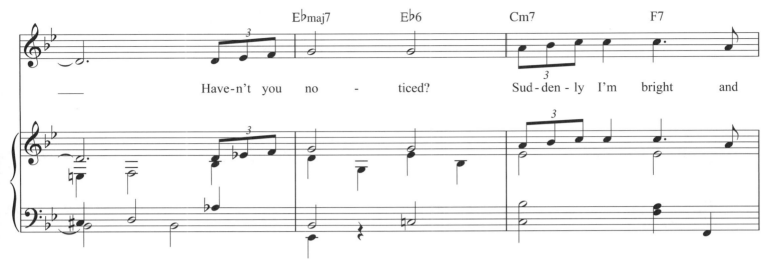

Have-n't you no - ticed? Sud-den-ly I'm bright and

breez - y ___ Be - cause of all the beau-ti - ful and new

things I'm learn-ing a-bout you day by

day. ___ Get-ting to day. ___

# GOODNIGHT, MY SOMEONE

from Meredith Willson's THE MUSIC MAN

By MEREDITH WILLSON

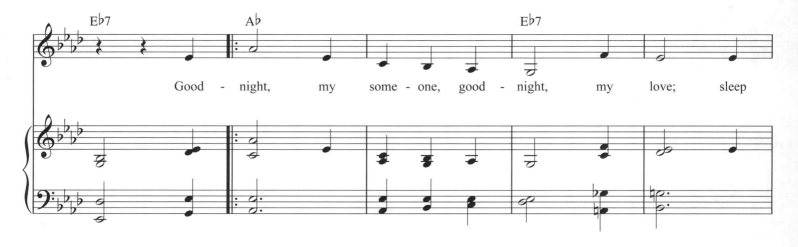

Good - night, my some - one, good - night, my love; sleep

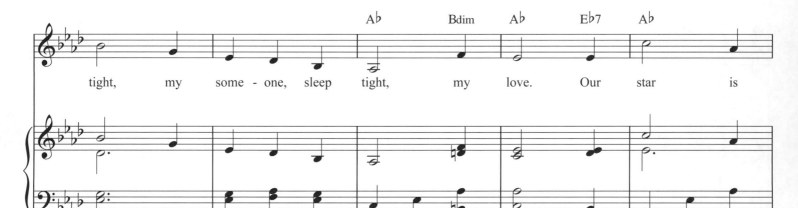

tight, my some - one, sleep tight, my love. Our star is

shin - ing its bright - est light for good - night, my love, for good -

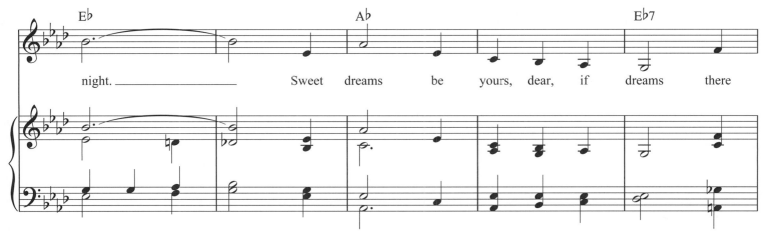

night. _____ Sweet dreams be yours, dear, if dreams there

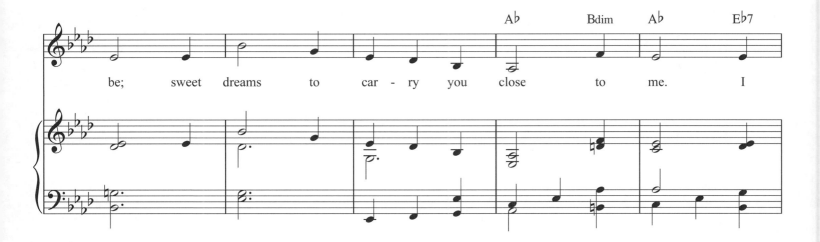

be; sweet dreams to car - ry you close to me. I

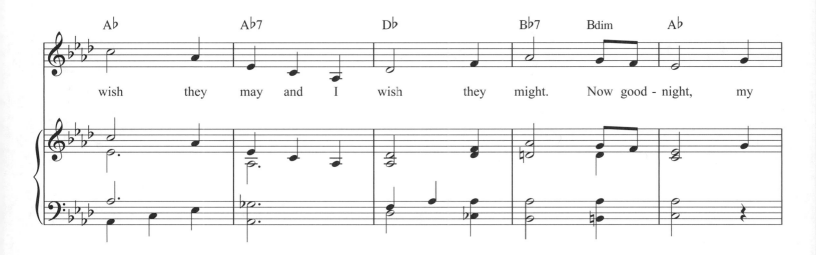

wish they may and I wish they might. Now good - night, my

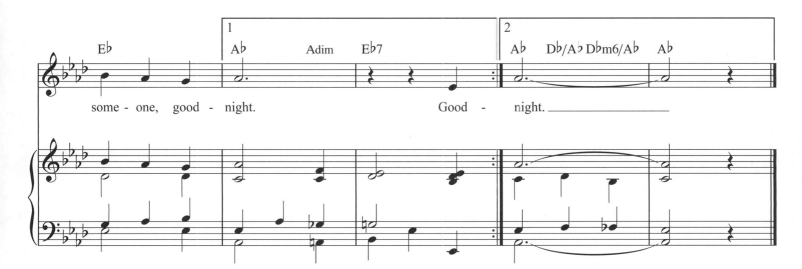

some - one, good - night. Good - night. _____

# I COULD HAVE DANCED ALL NIGHT

from MY FAIR LADY

Words by ALAN JAY LERNER
Music by FREDERICK LOEWE

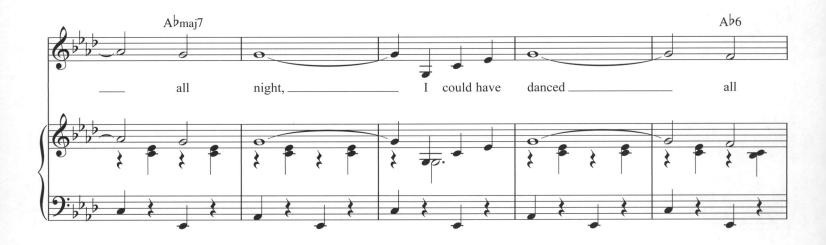

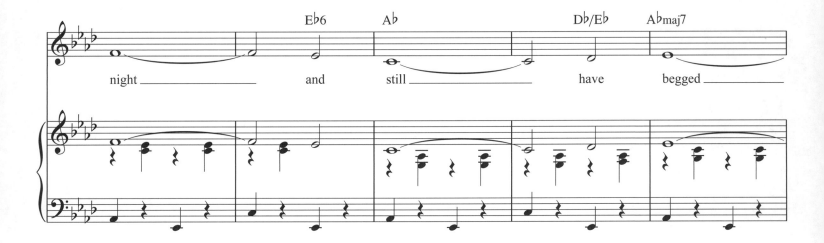

73

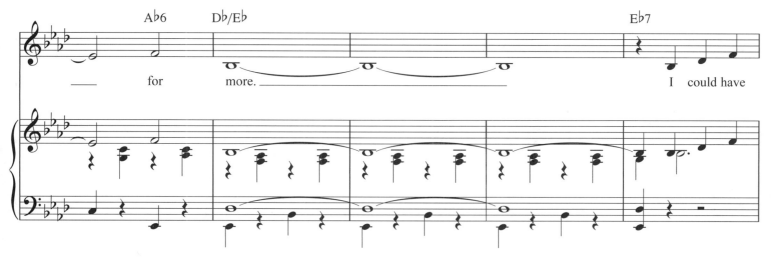

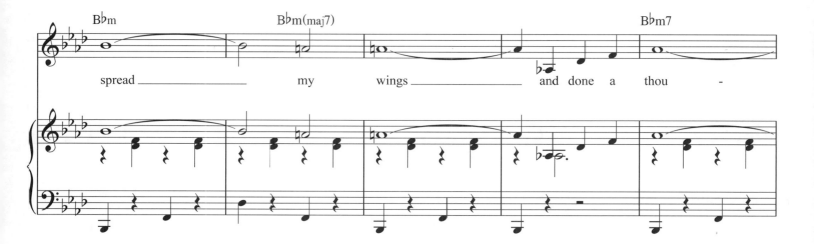

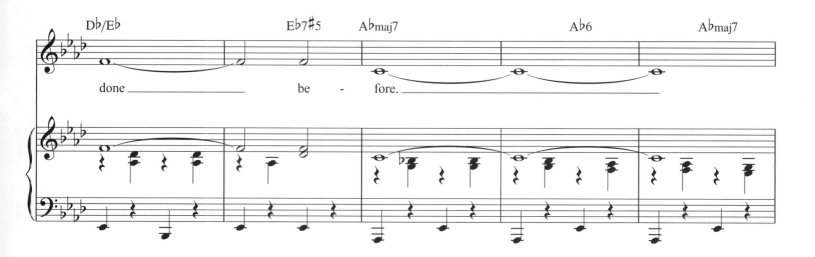

74

I'll nev - er know _____ what made it so _____ ex -
cit - ing, _____ why all at once _____ _____ my heart took flight. _____

_____ I on - ly know _____ when he _____

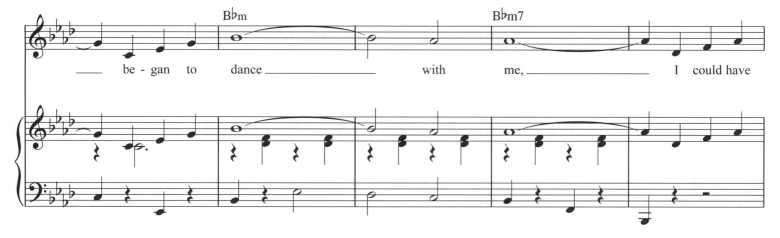

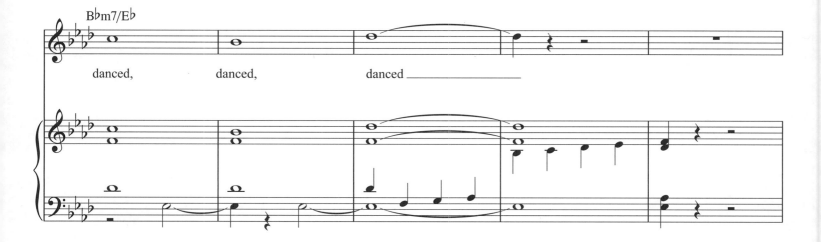

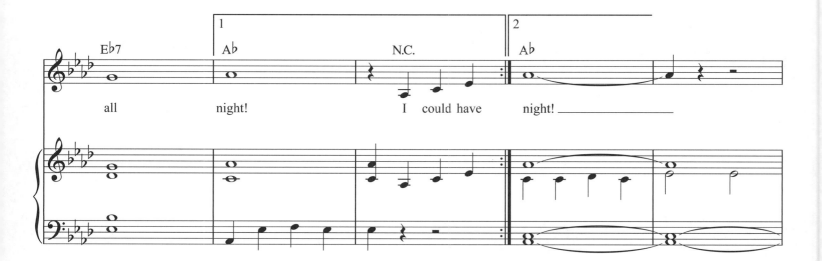

# I DON'T KNOW HOW TO LOVE HIM

## from JESUS CHRIST SUPERSTAR

Words by TIM RICE
Music by ANDREW LLOYD WEBBER

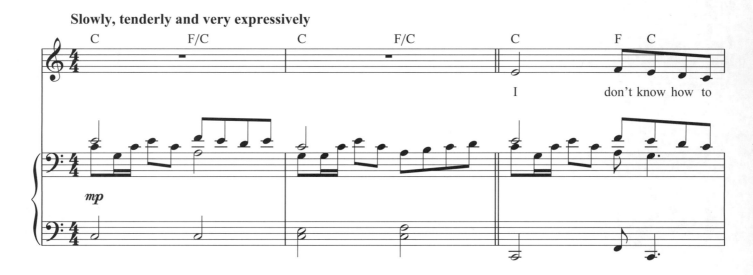

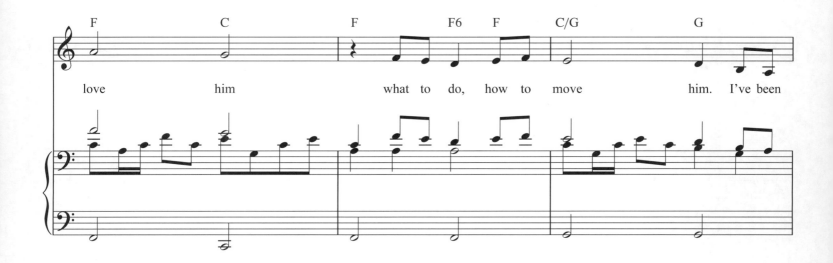

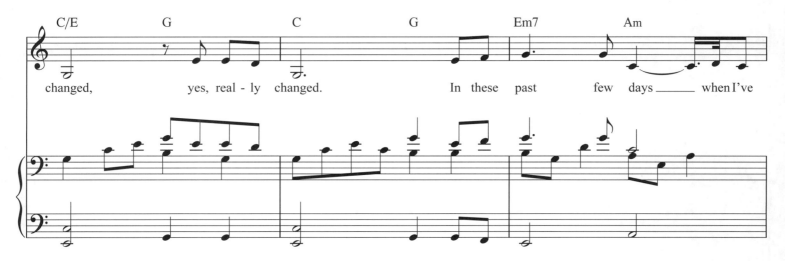

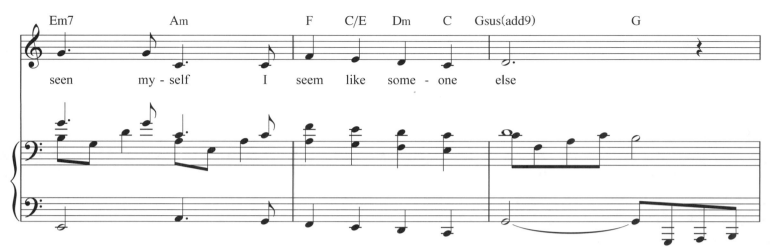

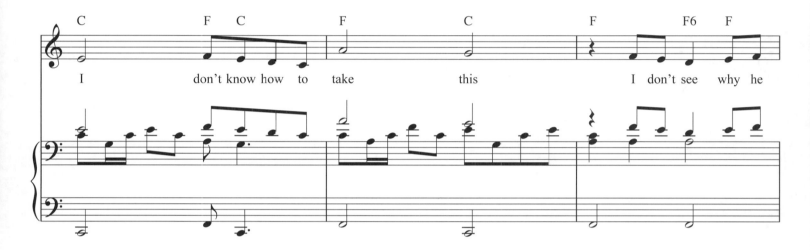

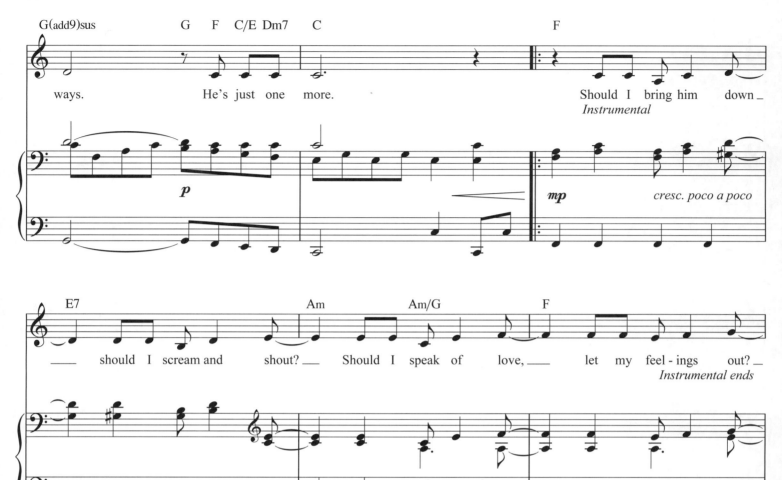

ways. He's just one more. Should I bring him down _

should I scream and shout? _ Should I speak of love, _ let my feel - ings out? _

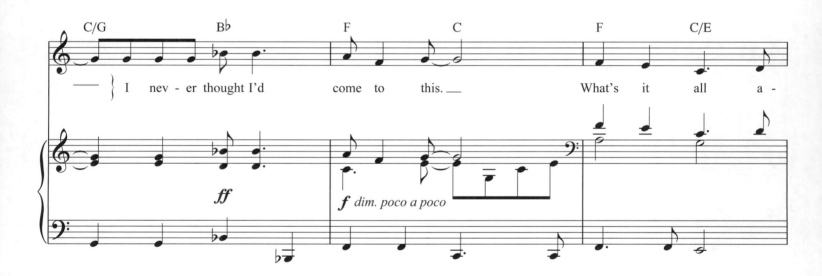

— I nev - er thought I'd come to this. _ What's it all a -

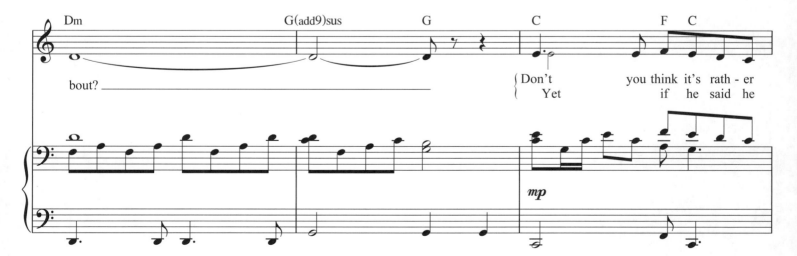

bout? _ Don't you think it's rath - er
Yet if he said he

fun - ny
loved me,

I should be in this po - si - tion? I'm the
I'd be lost I'd be fright - ened. I could-n't

one
cope

who's al - ways been
just could-n't cope

So calm and cool
I'd turn my head

no lov-er's fool
I'd back a - way

run - ning ev - 'ry show.
I would-n't want to know.

He scares me
He scares me

1
C

so. _____

2
C

so

I want him so.

I love him so.

# I DREAMED A DREAM
## from LES MISÉRABLES

Music by CLAUDE-MICHEL SCHÖNBERG
Lyrics by ALAIN BOUBLIL, JEAN-MARC NATEL
and HERBERT KRETZMER

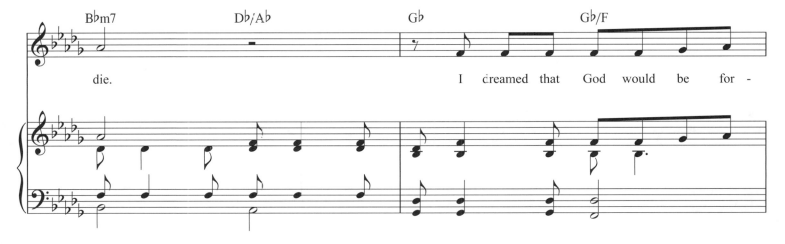

die. I dreamed that God would be for-

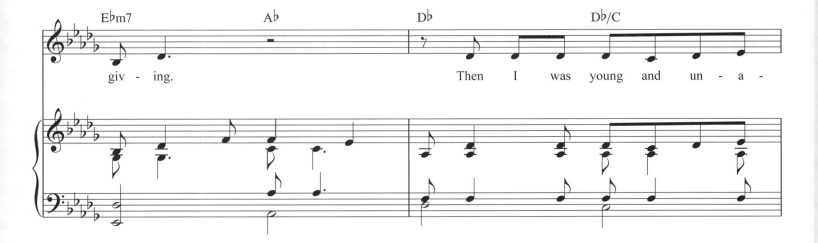

giv - ing. Then I was young and un-a-

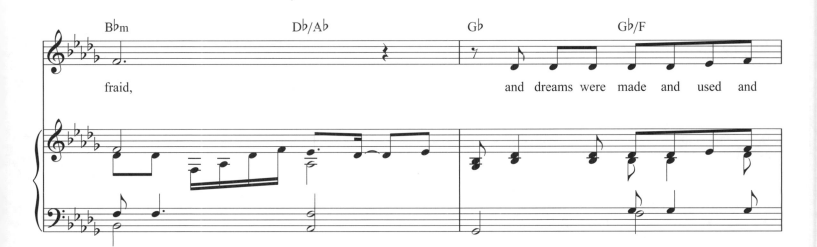

fraid, and dreams were made and used and

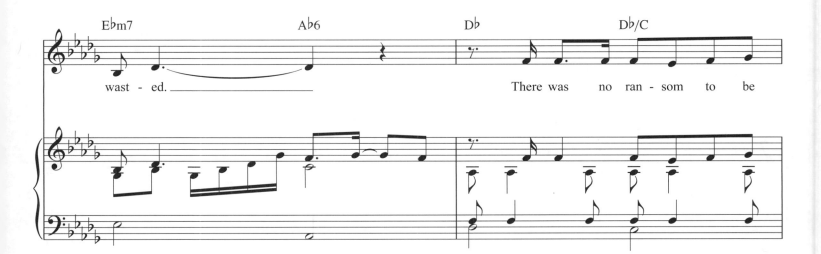

wast - ed. There was no ran - som to be

paid, no song un-sung, no wine un-tast-ed.

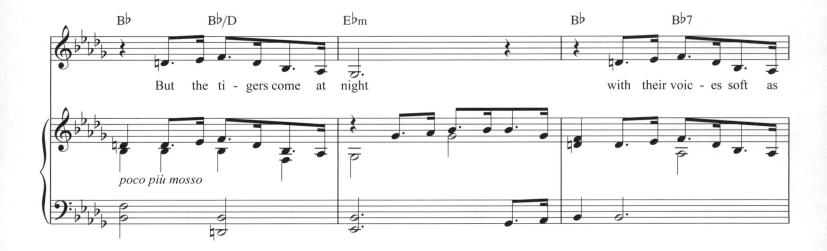

But the ti-gers come at night with their voic-es soft as

*poco più mosso*

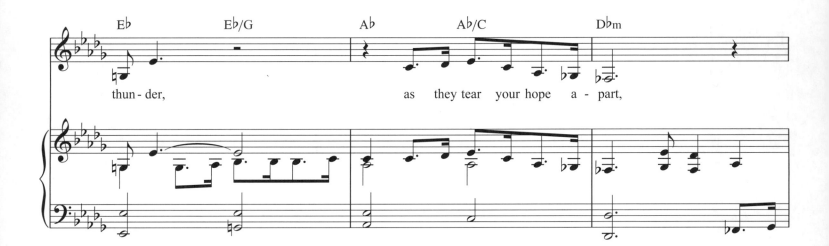

thun-der, as they tear your hope a-part,

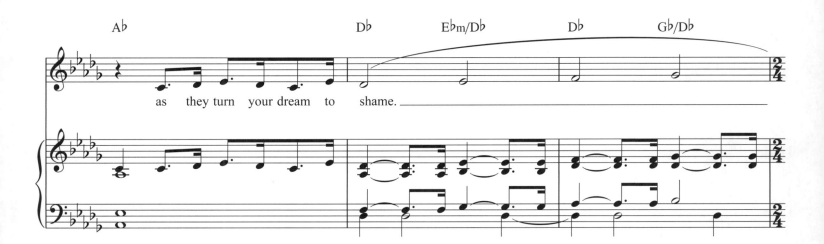

as they turn your dream to shame.

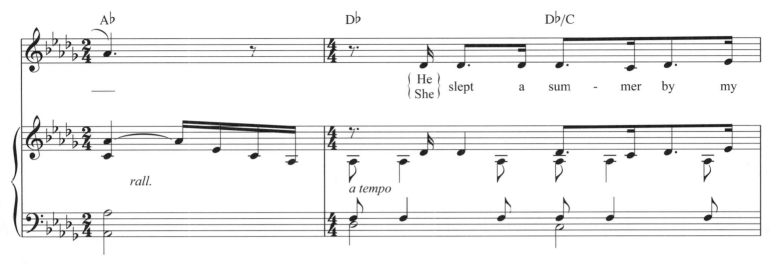

{He / She} slept a sum - mer by my

side. {He / She} filled my days with end - less won - der.

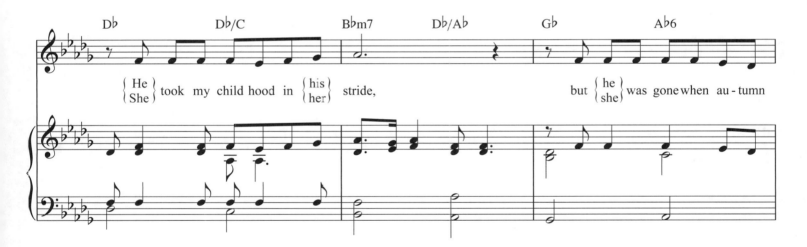

{He / She} took my child hood in {his / her} stride, but {he / she} was gone when au - tumn

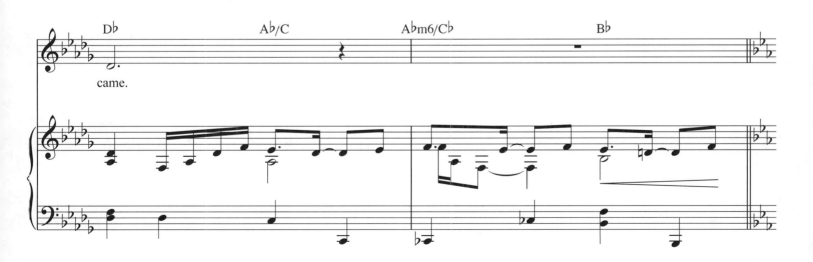

came.

# I FEEL PRETTY

## from WEST SIDE STORY

Lyrics by STEPHEN SONDHEIM
Music by LEONARD BERNSTEIN

Originally an ensemble number, adapted here as a solo.

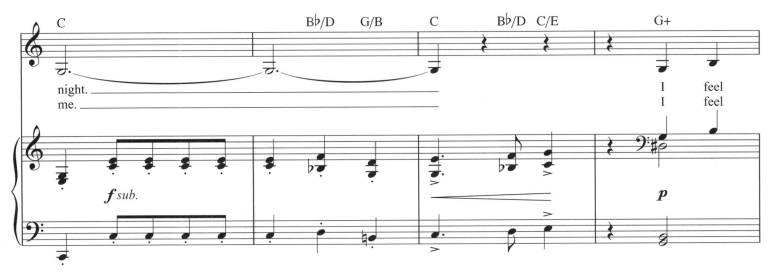

88

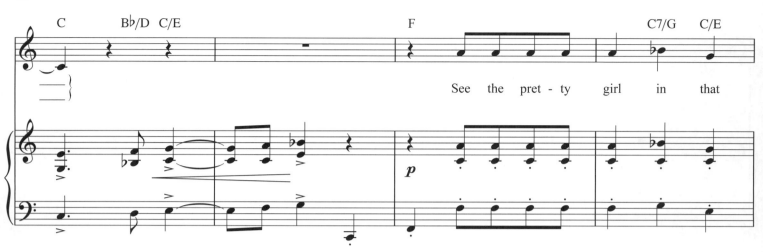

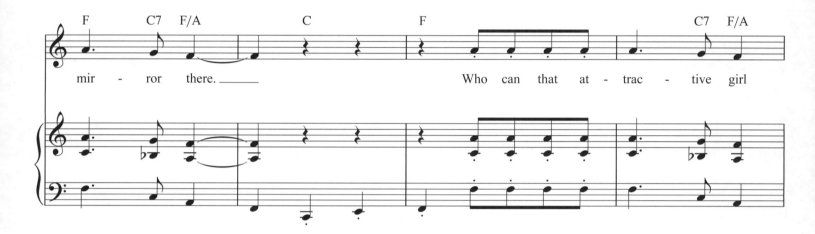

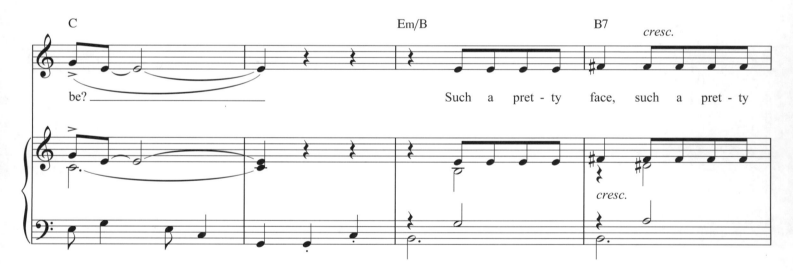

I feel stun - ning, and en - tranc - ing,

Feel like run - ning and danc - ing for joy, For I'm

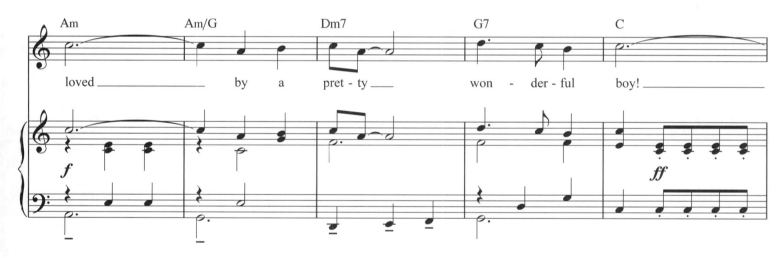

loved by a pret - ty won - der - ful boy!

I feel

# IF EVER I WOULD LEAVE YOU

from CAMELOT

Words by ALAN JAY LERNER
Music by FREDERICK LOEWE

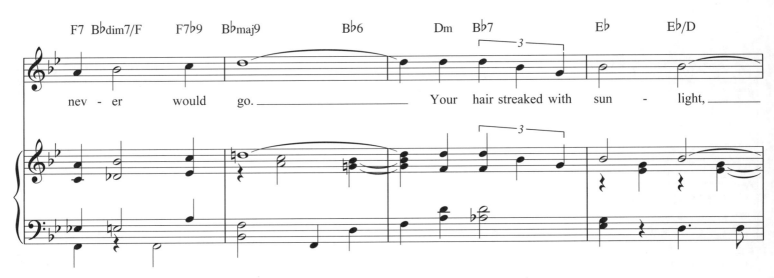

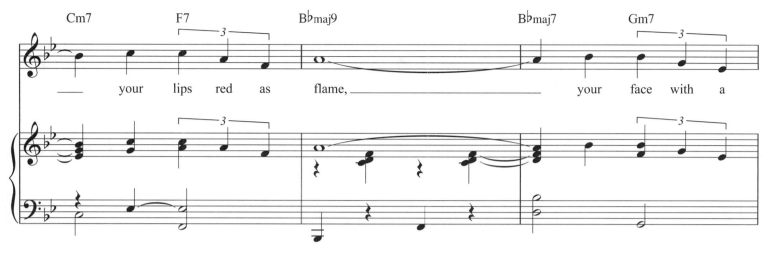

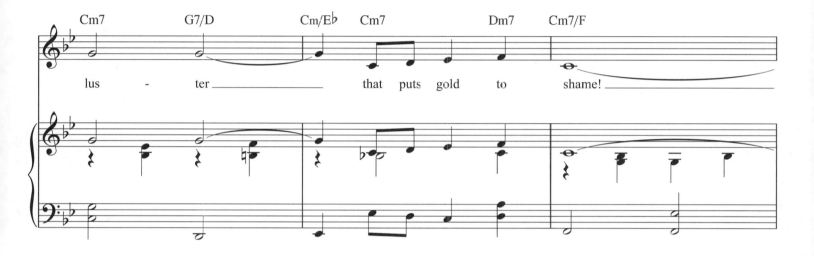

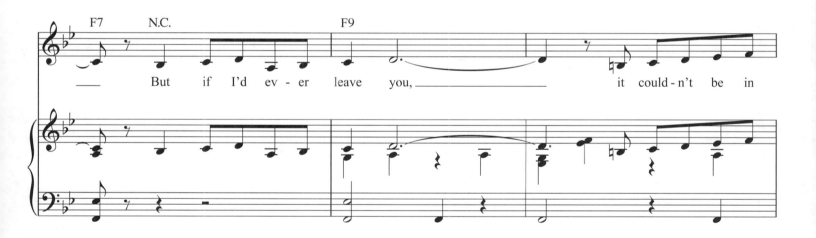

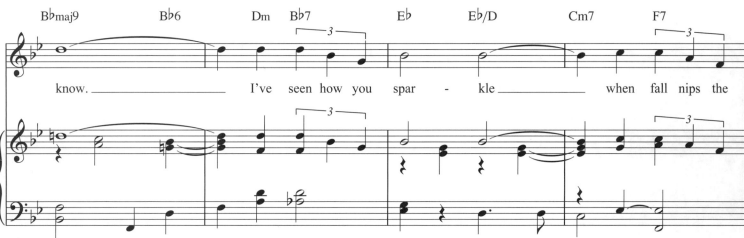

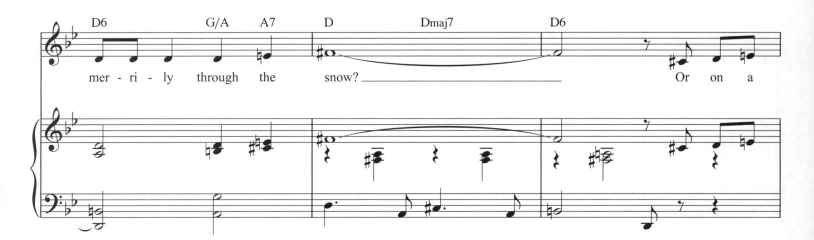

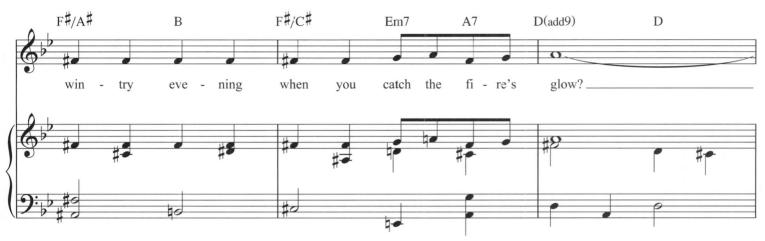

win - try eve - ning when you catch the fi - re's glow?_____

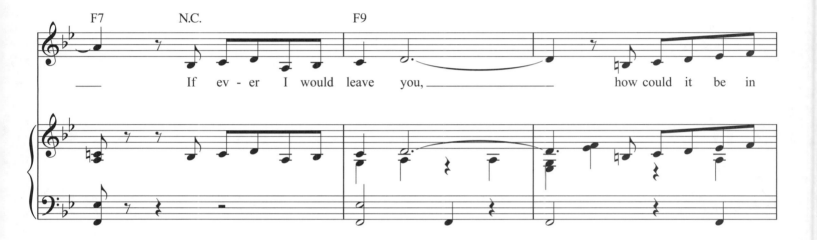

_____ If ev - er I would leave you,_____ how could it be in

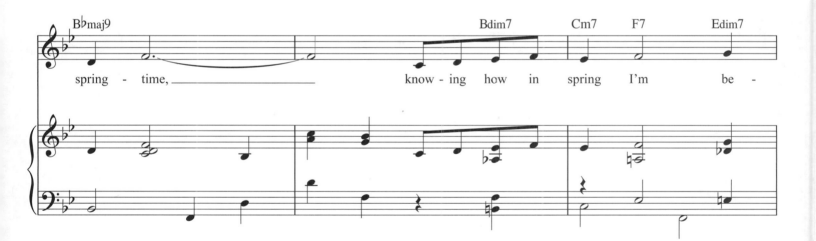

spring - time,_____ know - ing how in spring I'm be -

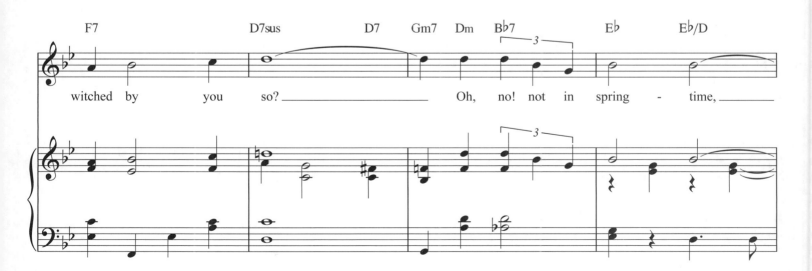

witched by you so?_____ Oh, no! not in spring - time,_____

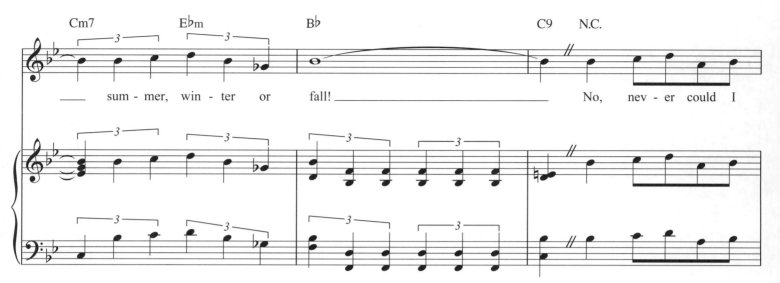

sum - mer, win - ter or fall! _____ No, nev - er could I

leave you _____ at all! _____ And could I

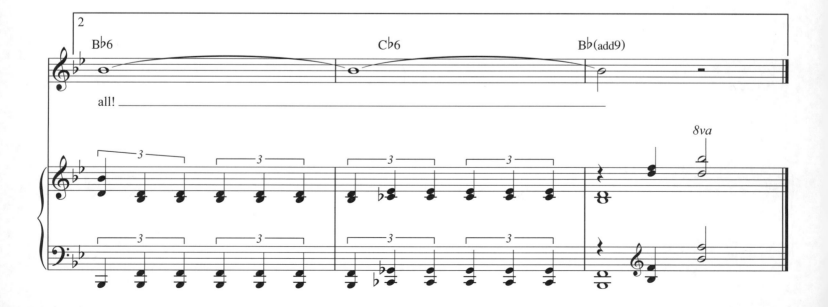

all! _____

# MAKE BELIEVE
## from SHOW BOAT

Lyrics by OSCAR HAMMERSTEIN II
Music by JEROME KERN

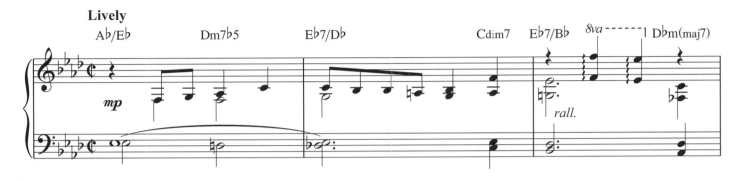

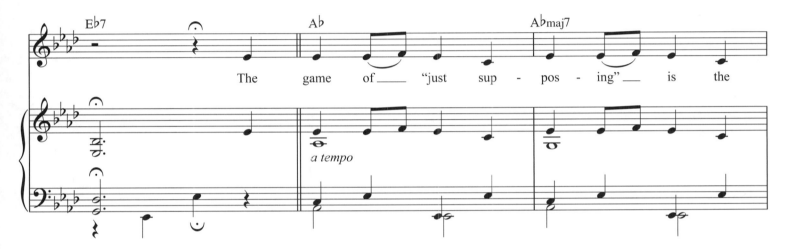

The game of ___ "just sup - pos - ing" ___ is the

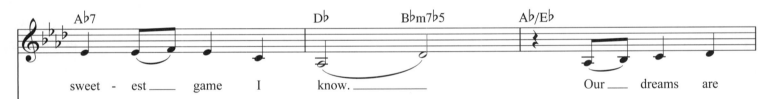

sweet - est ___ game I know. ___ Our ___ dreams are

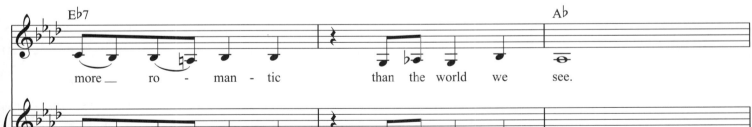

more ___ ro - man - tic than the world we see.

And if the things we dream a - bout don't hap - pen to be

so, _____ that's _ just an un - im - por - tant

tech - ni - cal - i - ty. _____ We could

**Slower**

make be - lieve _____ I love you, _____ on - ly

make be - lieve _____ that you love me. _____ Oth - ers

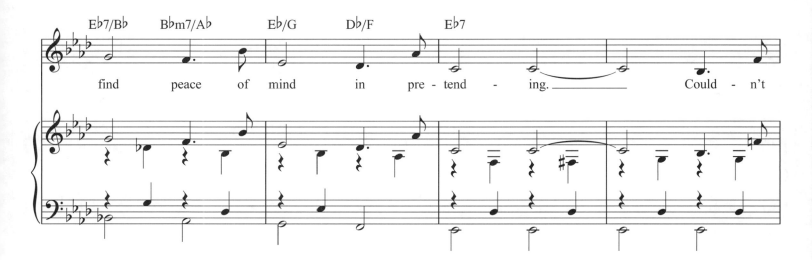

find peace of mind in pre - tend - ing. _____ Could - n't

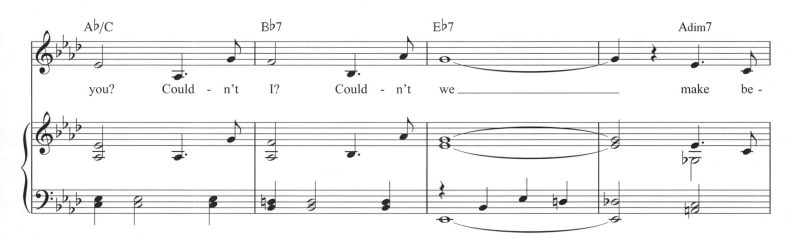

you? Could - n't I? Could - n't we _____ make be -

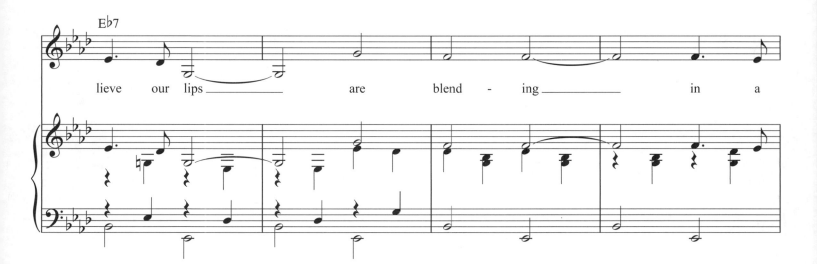

lieve our lips _____ are blend - ing _____ in a

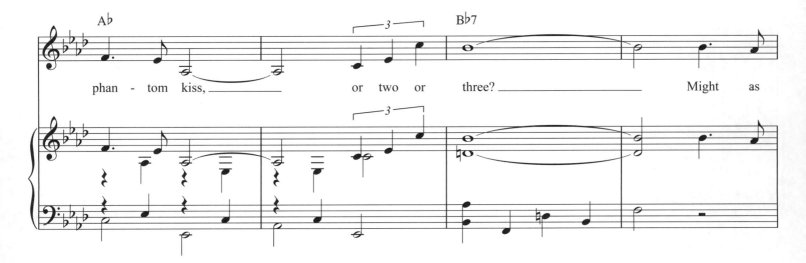

phan - tom kiss, _____ or two or three? _____ Might as

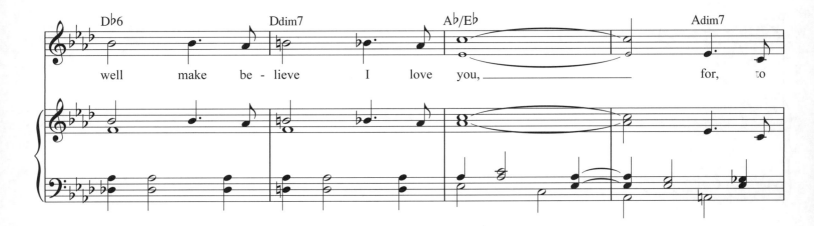

well make be - lieve I love you, _____ for, to

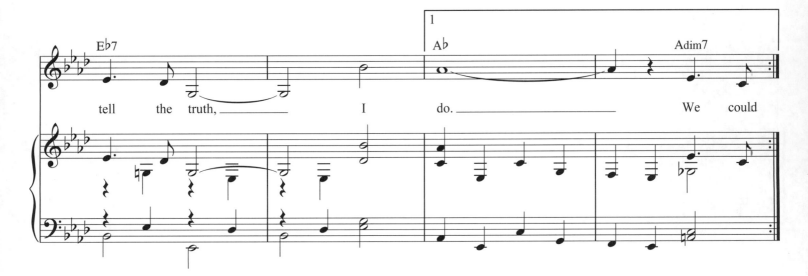

tell the truth, _____ I do. _____ We could

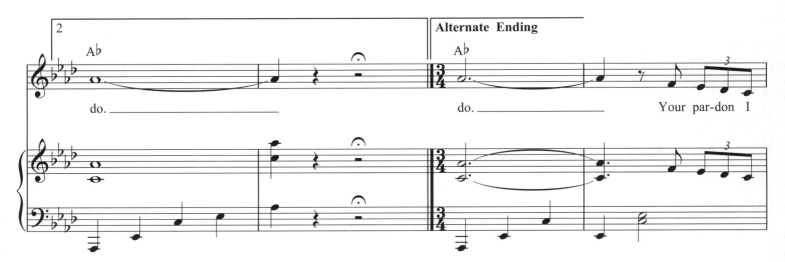

do. _____

**Alternate Ending**

do. _____ Your par-don I

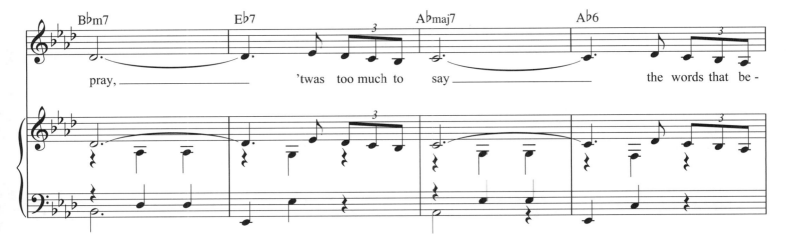

pray, _____ 'twas too much to say _____ the words that be -

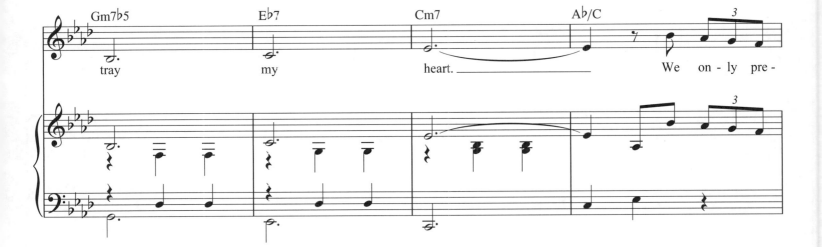

tray my heart. _____ We on - ly pre -

tend, _____ you do not of - fend _____ in play-ing a

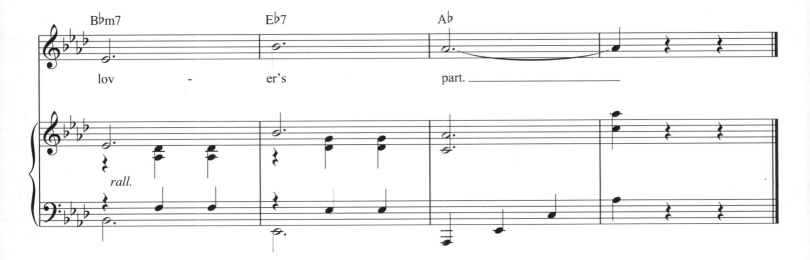

lov - er's part. _____

# IF I LOVED YOU
## from CAROUSEL

Lyrics by OSCAR HAMMERSTEIN II
Music by RICHARD RODGERS

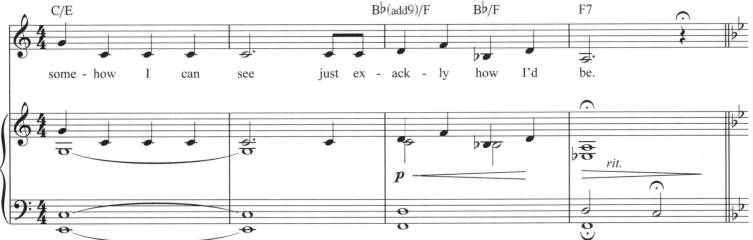

**Refrain** *(with great warmth, slowly)*

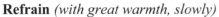

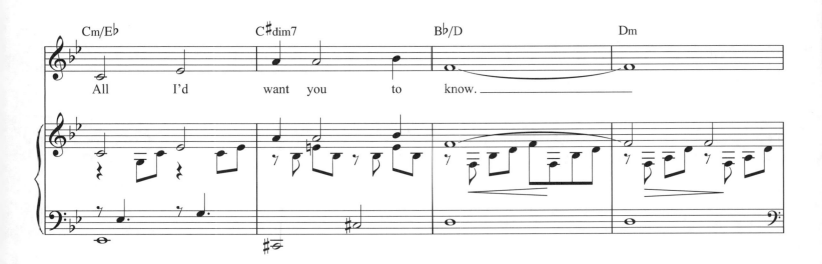

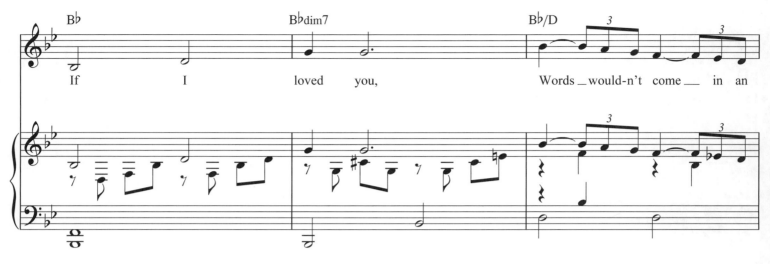

If I loved you, Words would-n't come in an

eas-y way, 'Round in cir-cles I'd go.

Long-in' to tell you, but a-fraid and

shy, I'd let my gold-en chanc-es pass me

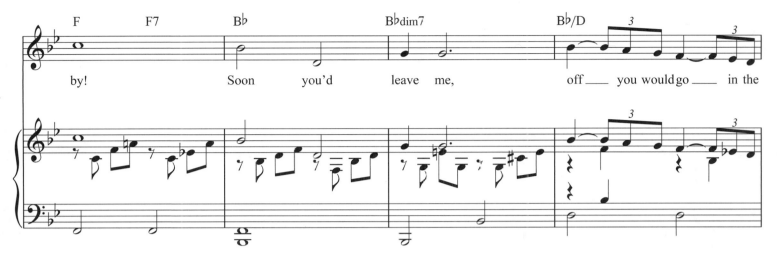

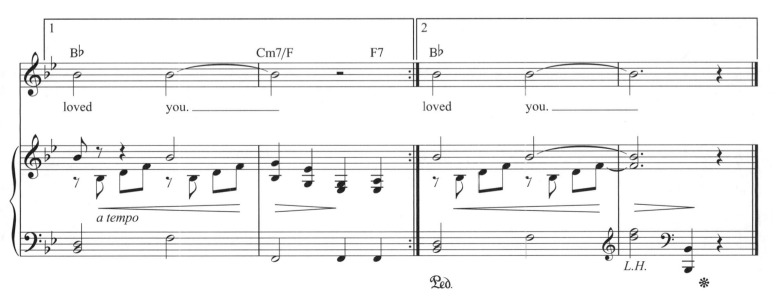

# THE IMPOSSIBLE DREAM
## (The Quest)
### from MAN OF LA MANCHA

Lyric by JOE DARION
Music by MITCH LEIGH

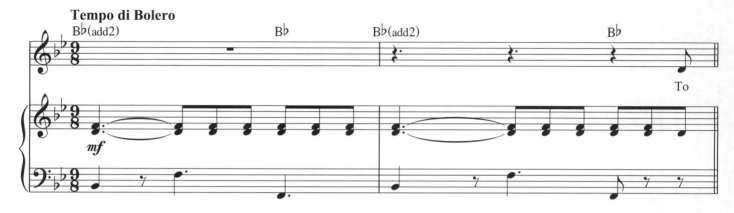

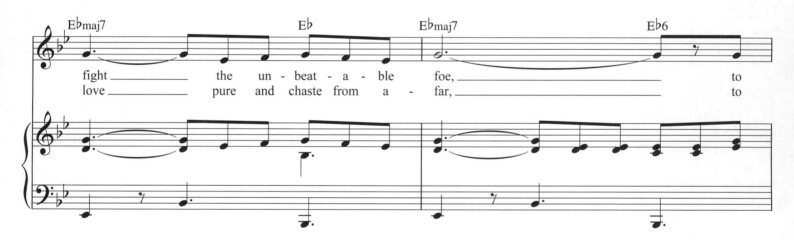

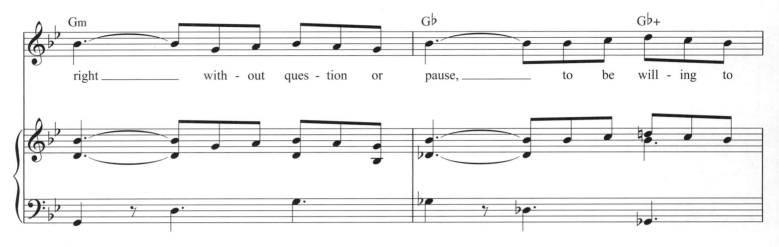

right _____ with - out ques - tion or pause, _____ to be will - ing to

march in - to hell for a heav - en - ly cause! And I know, _____ if I'll on - ly be

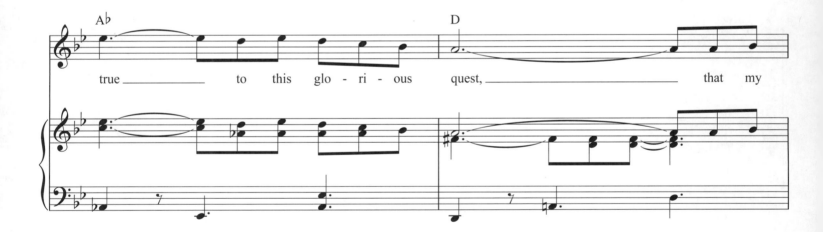

true _____ to this glo - ri - ous quest, _____ that my

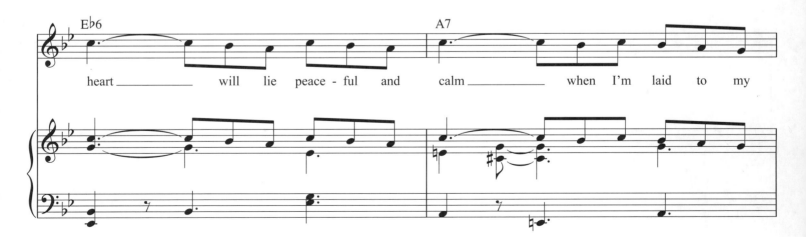

heart _____ will lie peace - ful and calm _____ when I'm laid to my

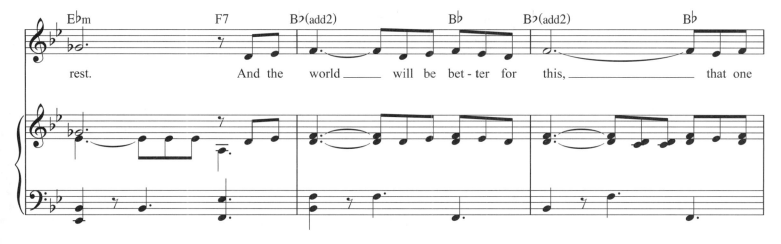

rest. And the world _____ will be bet-ter for this, _____ that one

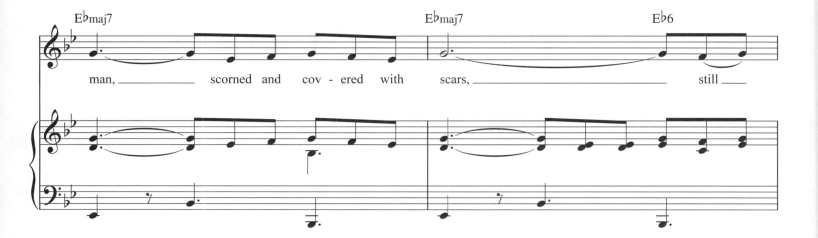

man, _____ scorned and cov-ered with scars, _____ still _____

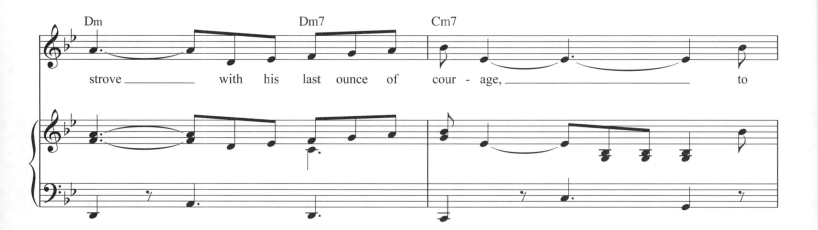

strove _____ with his last ounce of cour-age, _____ to

reach _____ the un-reach-a-ble stars. _____

*rall.*

# LUCK BE A LADY

## from GUYS AND DOLLS

By FRANK LOESSER

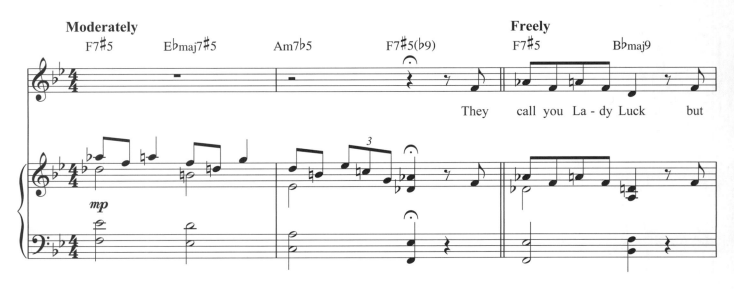

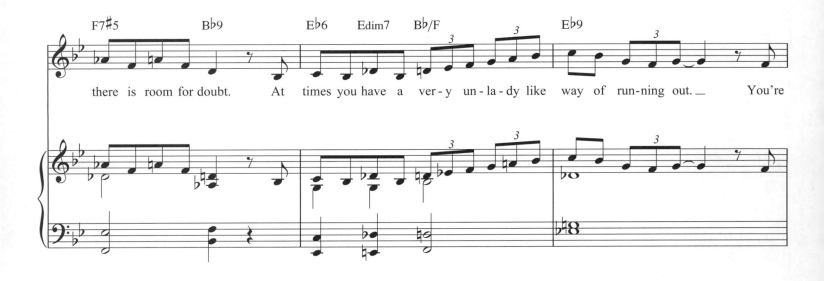

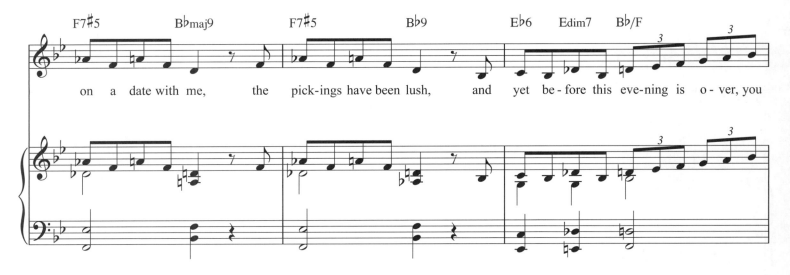

might give me the brush. \_\_ You might for-get your man-ners, you might re-fuse to stay, and

**Brightly, in 2**

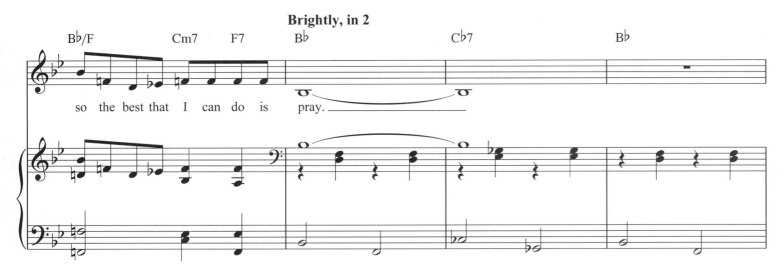

so the best that I can do is pray. _____

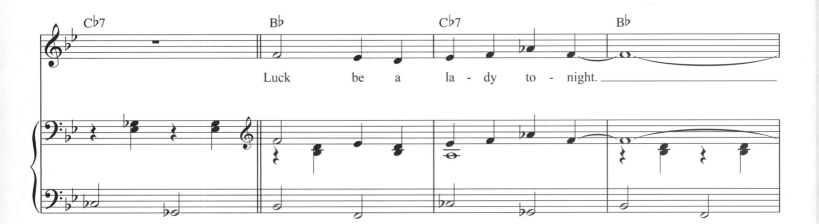

Luck be a la-dy to - night. _____

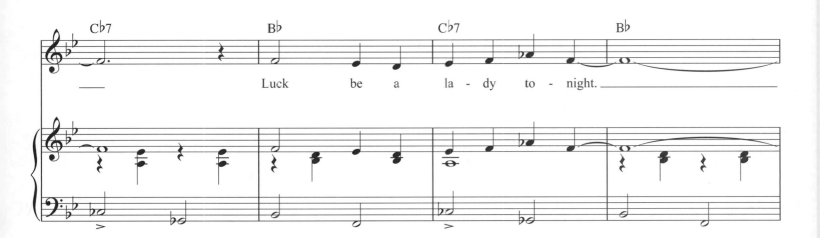

\_\_ Luck be a la-dy to - night. _____

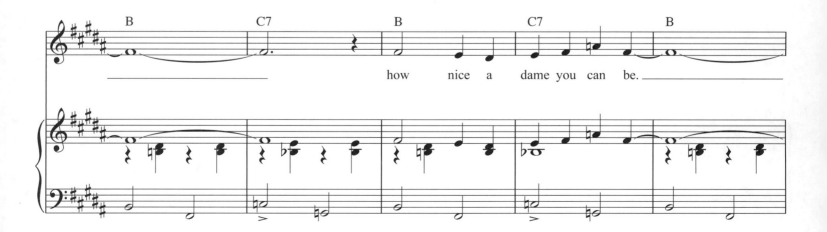

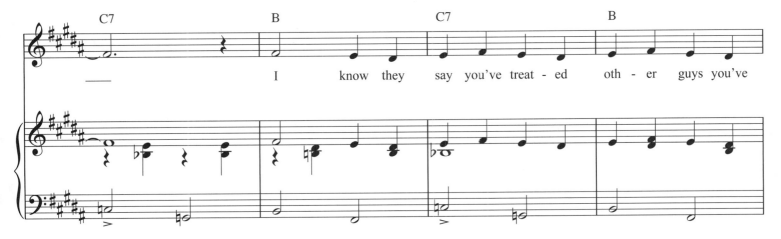

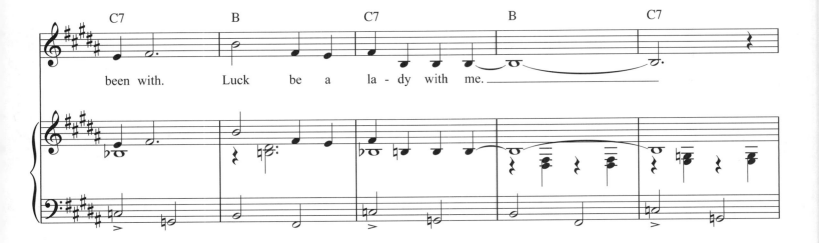

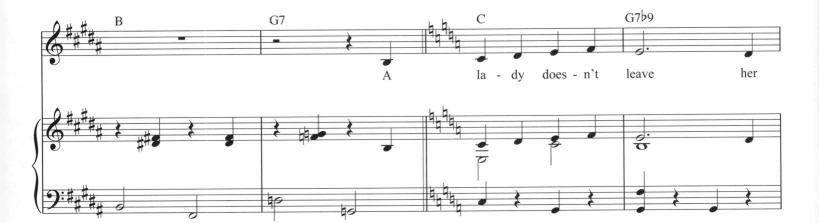

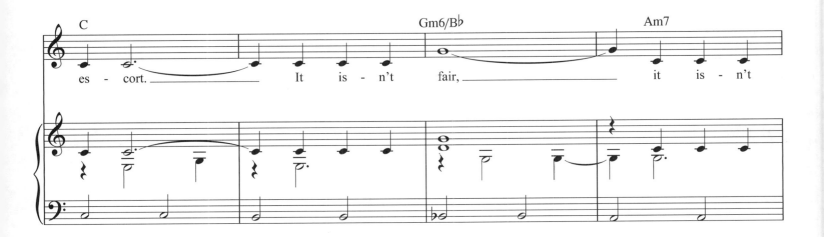

nice! _____ A la - dy does - n't wan - der all

o - ver the room and blow on some oth - er guy's dice. _____

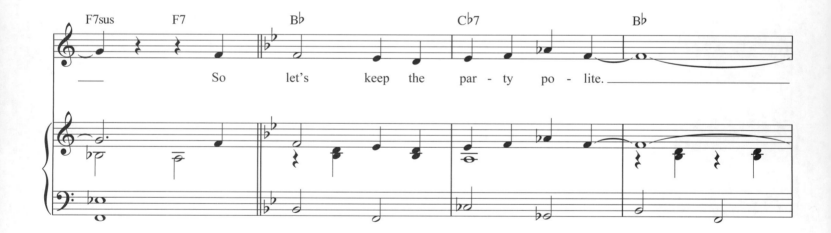

\_\_\_\_ So let's keep the par - ty po - lite. _____

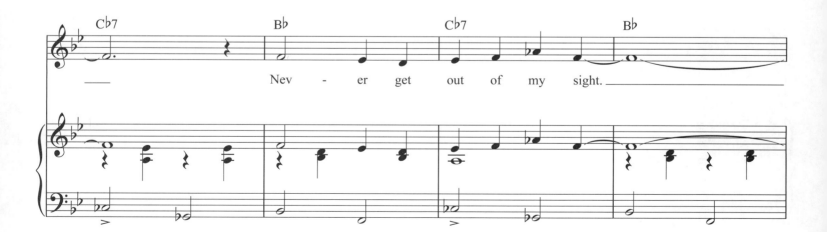

\_\_\_\_ Nev - er get out of my sight. _____

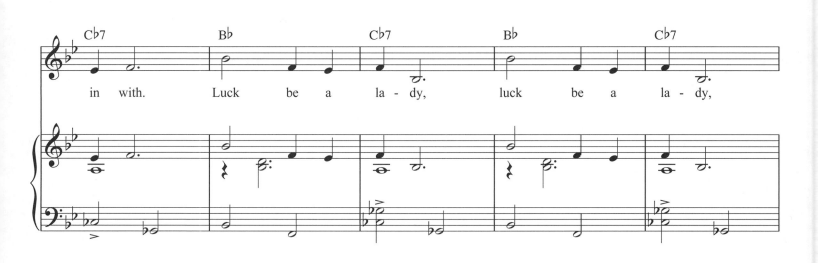

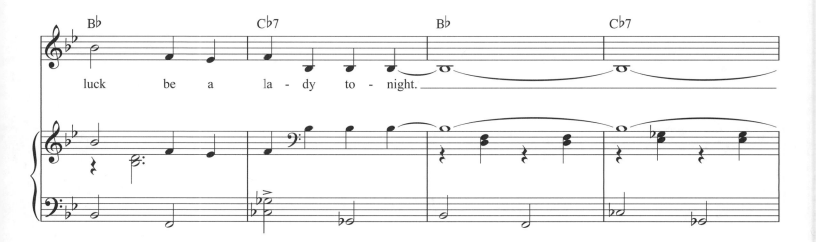

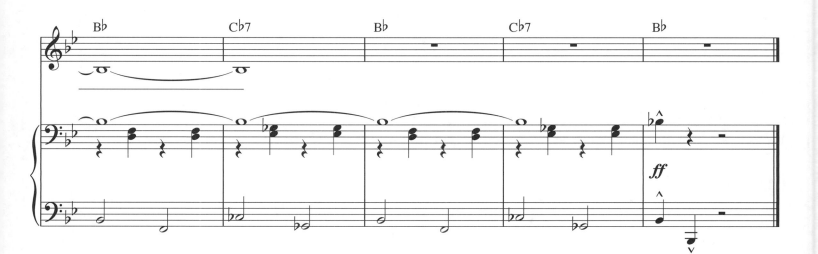

# THE MAN I LOVE

## from LADY BE GOOD
## from STRIKE UP THE BAND

Music and Lyrics by GEORGE GERSHWIN
and IRA GERSHWIN

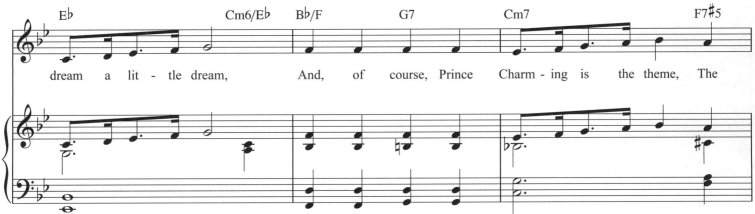

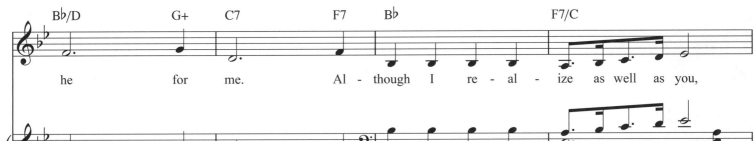

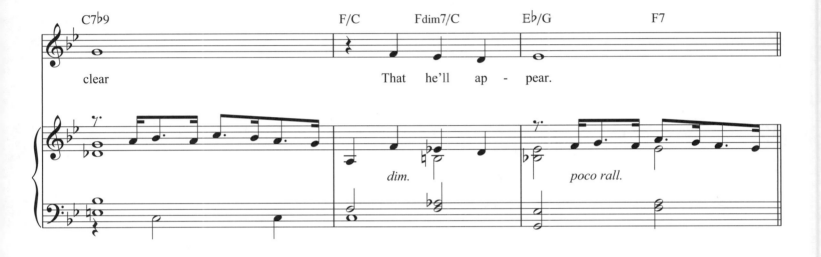

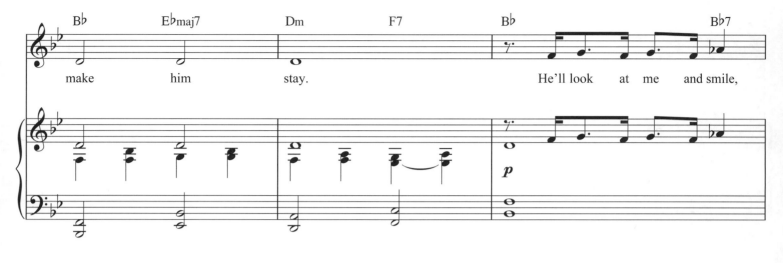

make him stay. He'll look at me and smile,

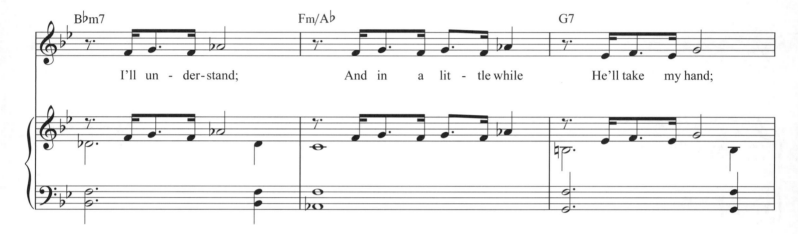

I'll un-der-stand; And in a lit-tle while He'll take my hand;

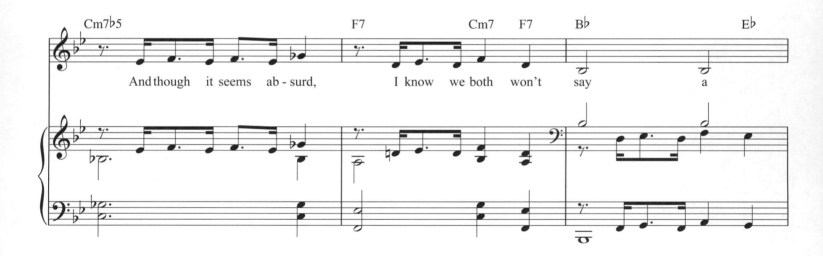

And though it seems ab-surd, I know we both won't say a

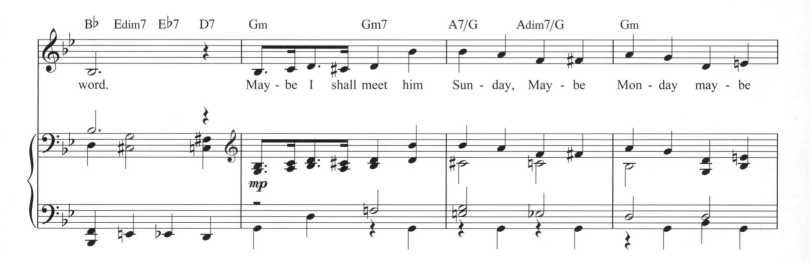

word. May-be I shall meet him Sun-day, May-be Mon-day may-be

# MATCHMAKER

## from the Musical FIDDLER ON THE ROOF

Words by SHELDON HARNICK
Music by JERRY BOCK

**Tempo di Valse**

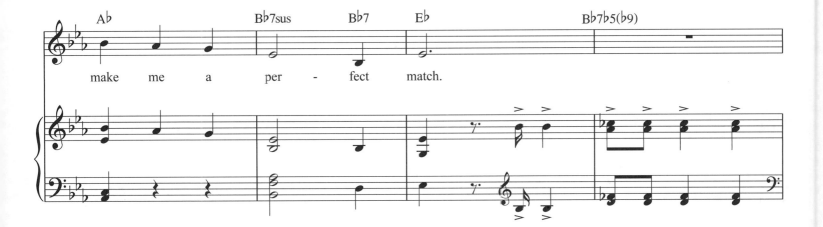

make me a per - fect match.

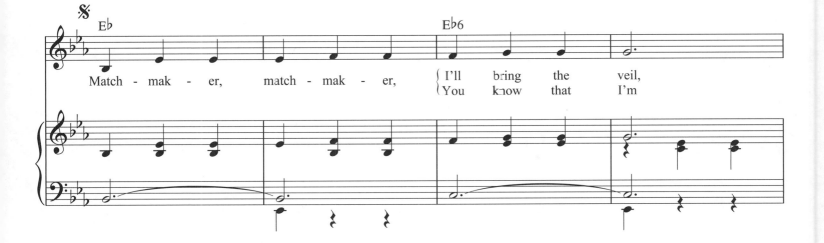

Match - mak - er, match - mak - er, I'll bring the veil, / You know that I'm

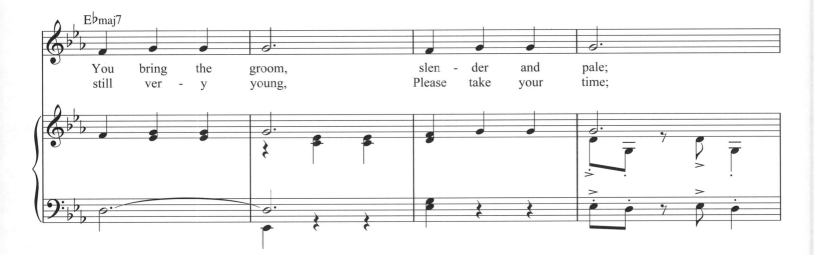

You bring the groom, slen - der and pale; / still ver - y young, Please take your time;

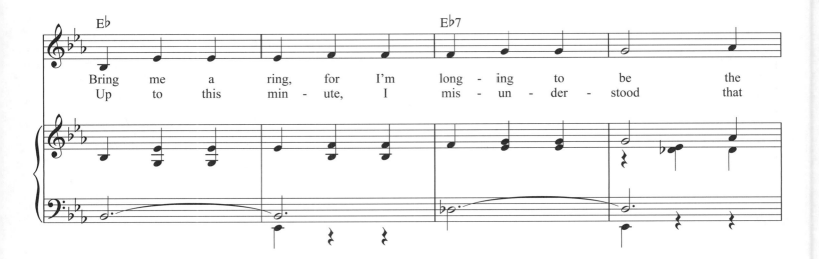

Bring me a ring, for I'm long - ing to be the / Up to this min - ute, I mis - un - der - stood that

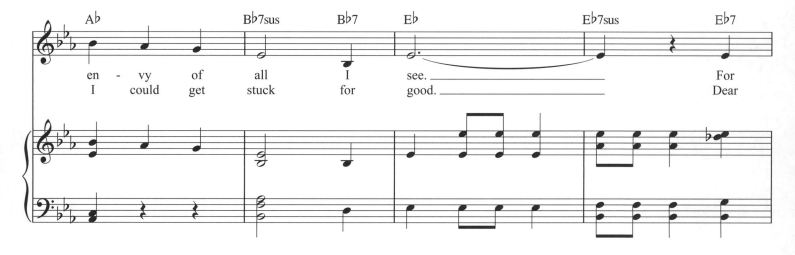

en - vy of all I see. _____ For
I could get all stuck for good. _____ Dear

Pop - pa, make him a schol - ar, For Mom -
Mom - ma, see that he's gen - tle, Re - mem -

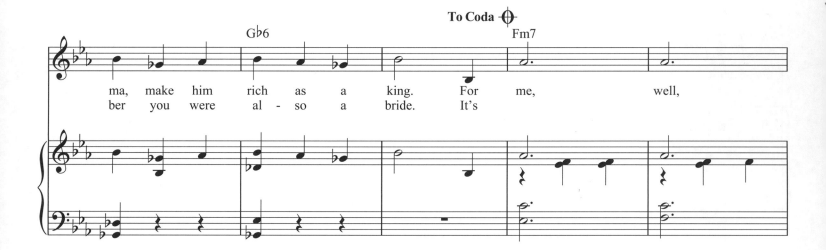

**To Coda** ⊕

ma, make him rich as a king. For me, well,
ber you were al - so a bride. It's

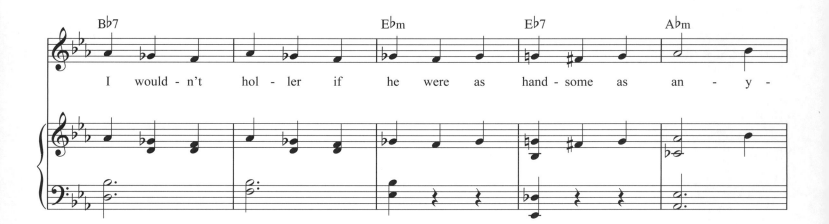

I would - n't hol - ler if he were as hand - some as an - y -

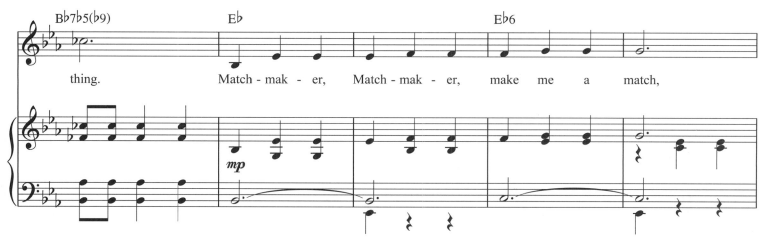

thing. Match - mak - er, Match - mak - er, make me a match,

Find me a find, catch me a catch; Night aft - er

night in the dark I'm a - lone, So find me a match

**D.S. al Coda**

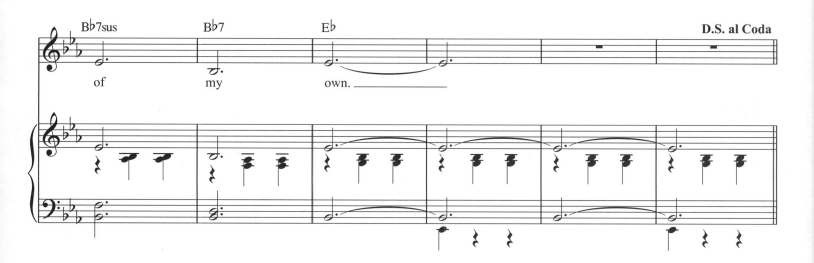

of my own. _____

**CODA**

not that I'm sen - ti - men - tal. It's

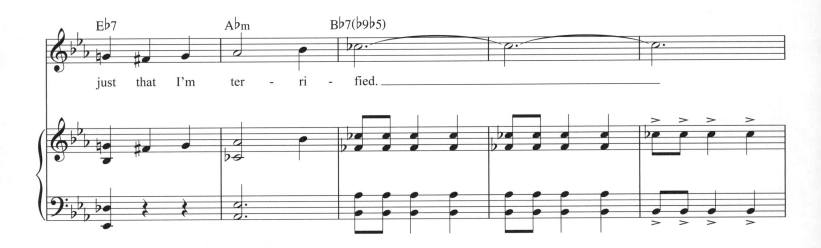

just that I'm ter - ri - fied.

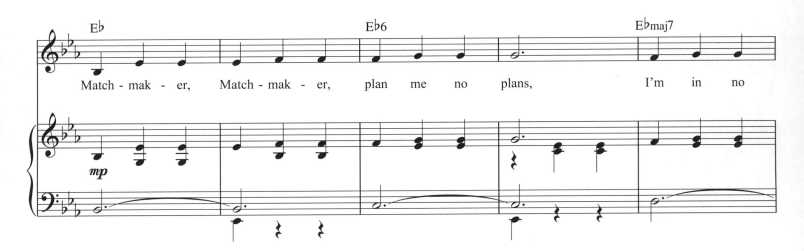

Match - mak - er, Match - mak - er, plan me no plans, I'm in no

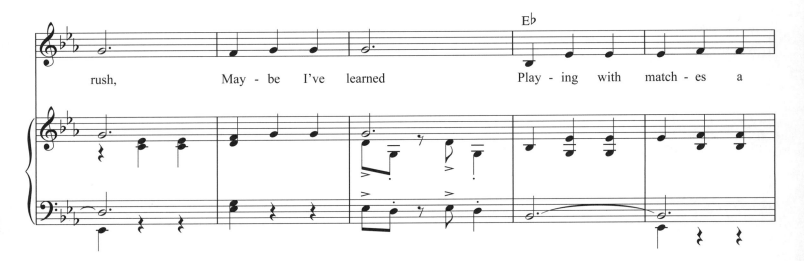

rush, May - be I've learned Play - ing with match - es a

123

girl can get burned. So bring me no ring, Groom me no

groom, Find me no find, Catch me no catch;

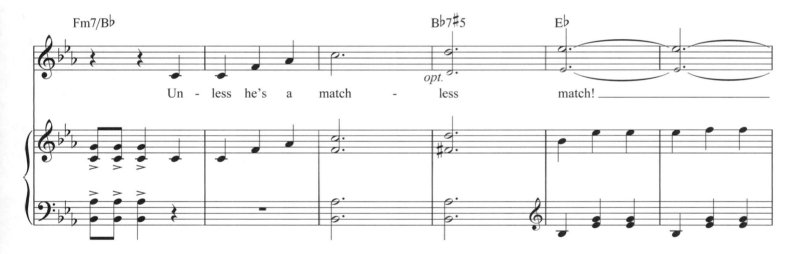

Un - less he's a match - less match! _____

# MEMORY
## from CATS

Music by ANDREW LLOYD WEBBER
Text by TREVOR NUNN after T.S. ELIOT

Mid - night. _____ Not a sound from the pave - ment. _____ Has the moon lost her
Mem - ory _____ all a - lone in the moon - light _____ I can smile at the

mem - o - ry? _____ She is smil-ing a - lone. _____ In the
old days, _____ I was beau-ti-ful then. _____ I re -

lamp - light the with-ered leaves col - lect at my feet
mem - ber the time I knew what hap-pi-ness was,
and the
let the

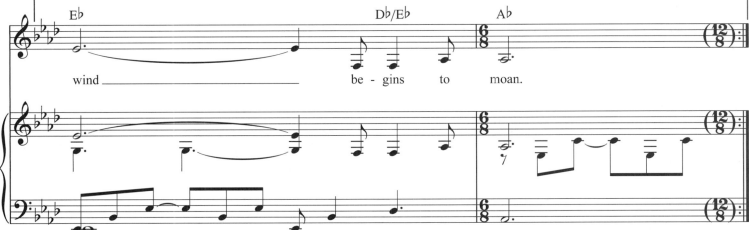

wind _____ be - gins to moan.

mem - ory live a - gain.

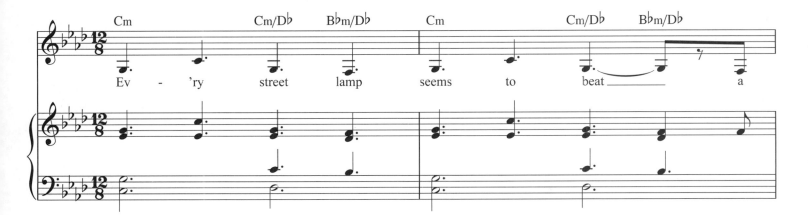

Ev - 'ry street lamp seems to beat _____ a

fa - tal - is - tic warn - ing.

Some - one mut - ters ___ and a street lamp gut - ters ___ and

soon it will be morn - ing.

Day - light. ___ I must wait for the sun - rise, ___ I must think of a

127

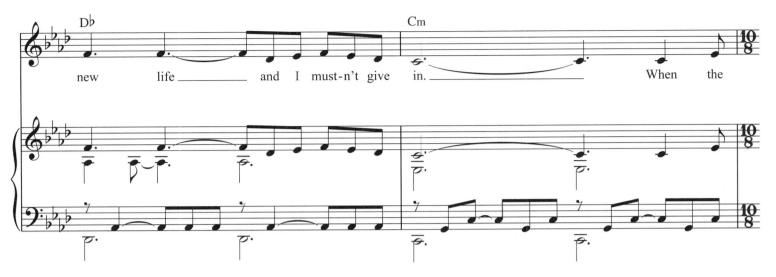

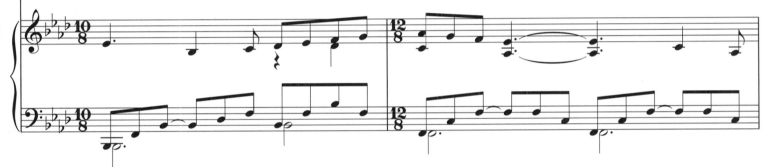

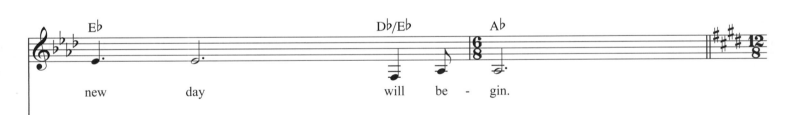

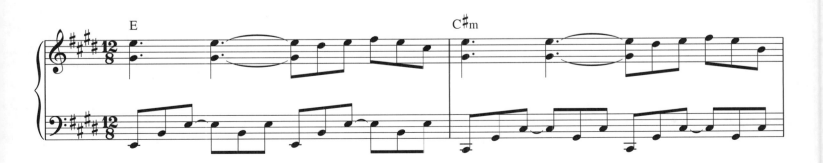

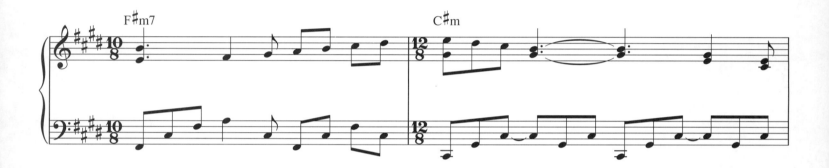

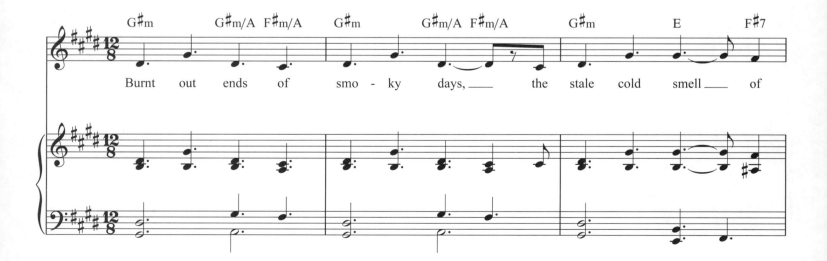

Burnt out ends of smo - ky days, ___ the stale cold smell ___ of

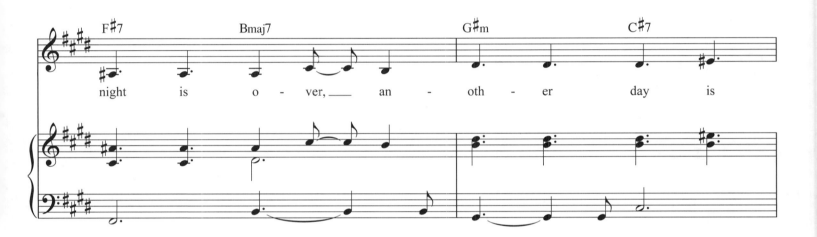

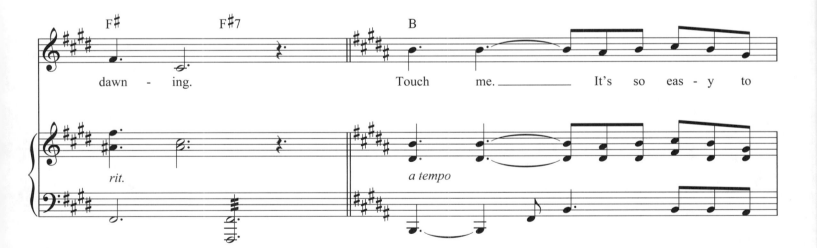

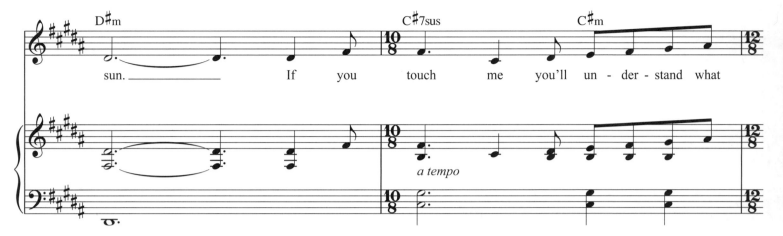

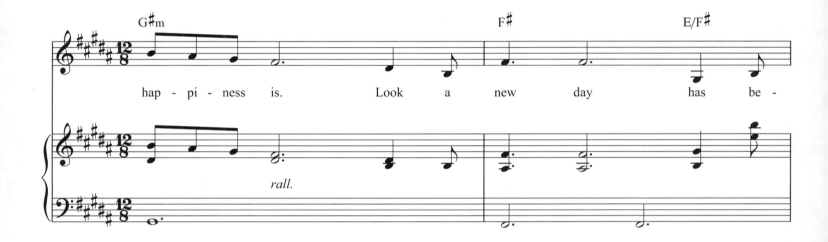

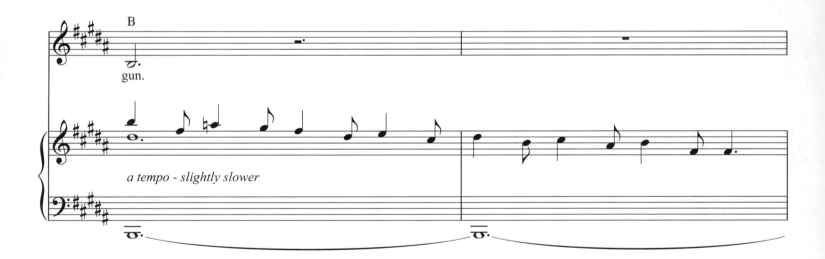

# NO ONE IS ALONE

## from INTO THE WOODS

Words and Music by
STEPHEN SONDHEIM

lone, tru - ly. No one is a - lone.

Some-times peo-ple leave you, _____ Half way through the wood.

*marcato*

Oth - ers may de - ceive you. _____ You de - cide what's good. _____

*marc.*

_____ You de - cide a - lone. But no one is a -

134

# MY FAVORITE THINGS

## from THE SOUND OF MUSIC

Lyrics by OSCAR HAMMERSTEIN II
Music by RICHARD RODGERS

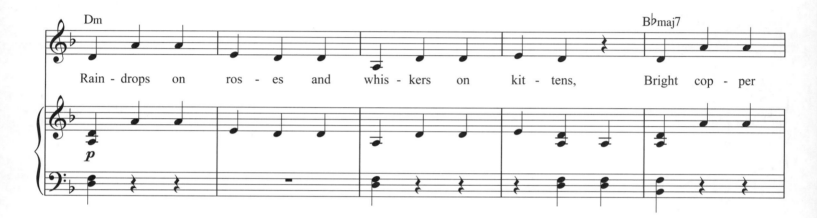

Rain - drops on ros - es and whis - kers on kit - tens, Bright cop - per

ket - tles and warm wool - en mit - tens, Brown pa - per pack - ag - es

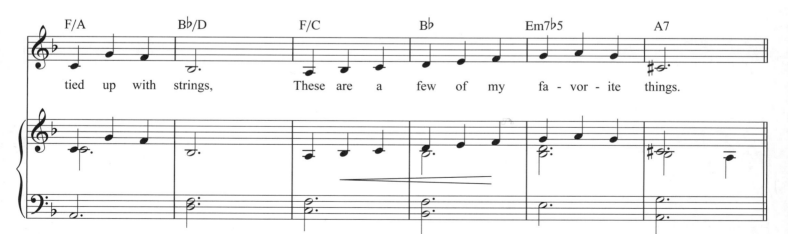

tied up with strings, These are a few of my fa - vor - ite things.

Girls in white dress - es with blue sat - in sash - es, Snow - flakes that

stay on my nose and eye - lash - es, Sil - ver white win - ters that

melt in - to springs, These are a few of my fa - vor - ite things.

When the dog bites, When the bee stings, When I'm

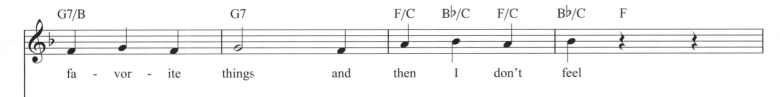

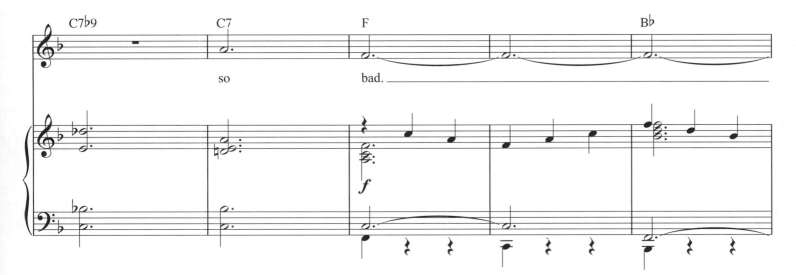

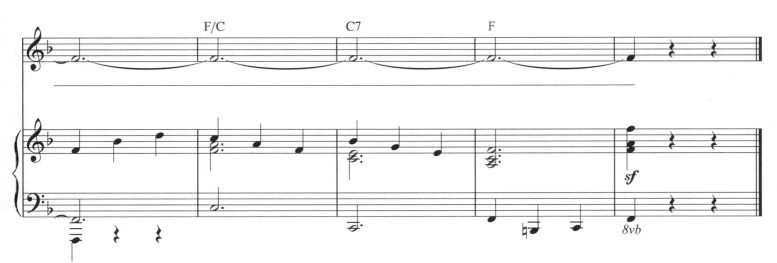

# MY FUNNY VALENTINE
## from BABES IN ARMS

Words by LORENZ HART
Music by RICHARD RODGERS

141

tent. Thou no - ble, up - right, truth - ful, sin - cere and slight - ly dop - ey

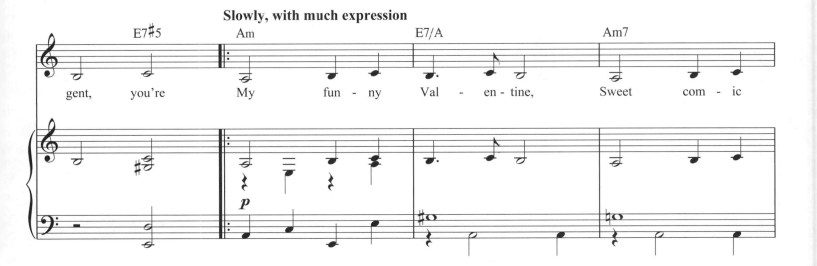

**Slowly, with much expression**

gent, you're My fun - ny Val - en - tine, Sweet com - ic

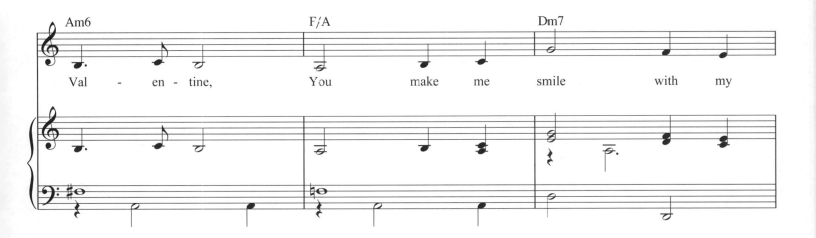

Val - en - tine, You make me smile with my

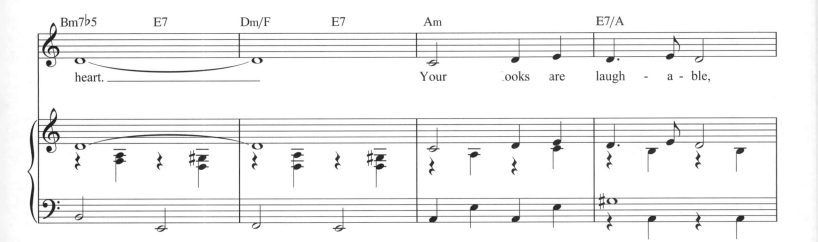

heart. _____ Your looks are laugh - a - ble,

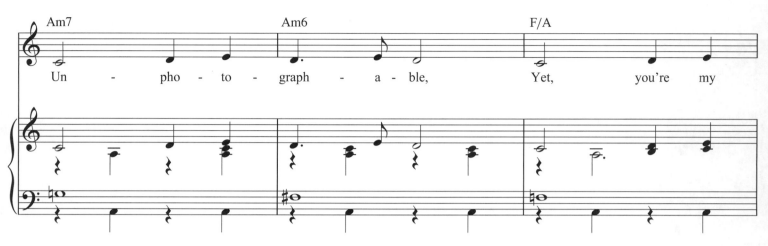

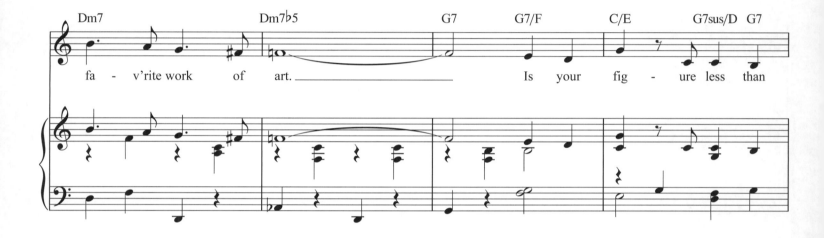

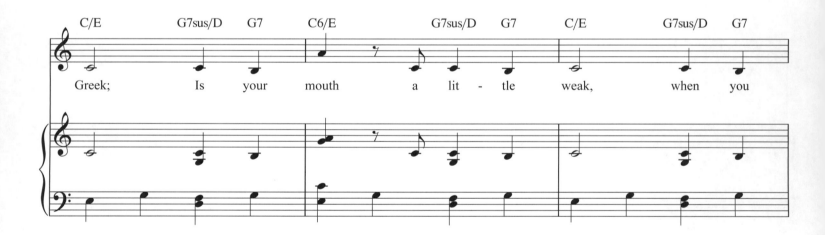

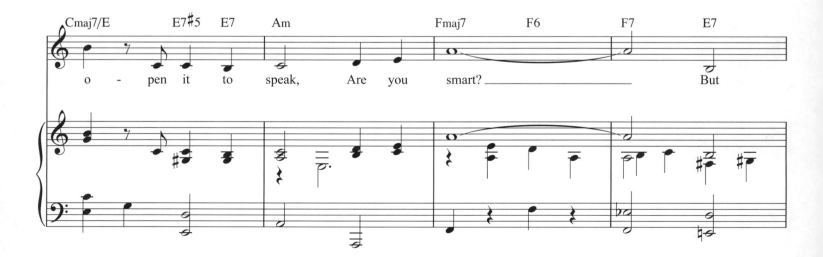

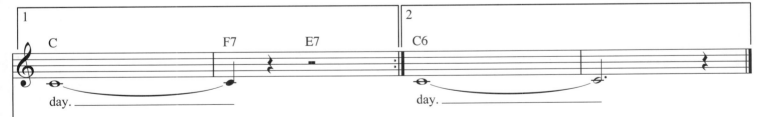

# OH, WHAT A BEAUTIFUL MORNIN'
## from OKLAHOMA!

Lyrics by OSCAR HAMMERSTEIN II
Music by RICHARD RODGERS

Moderate Waltz

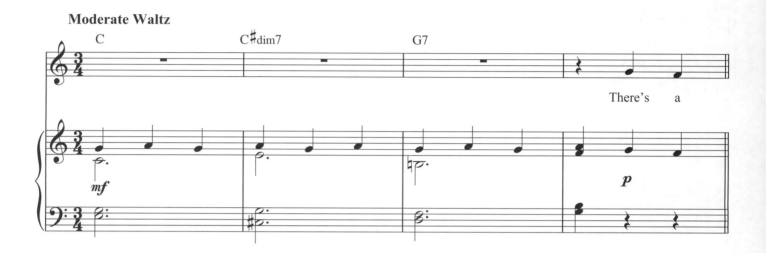

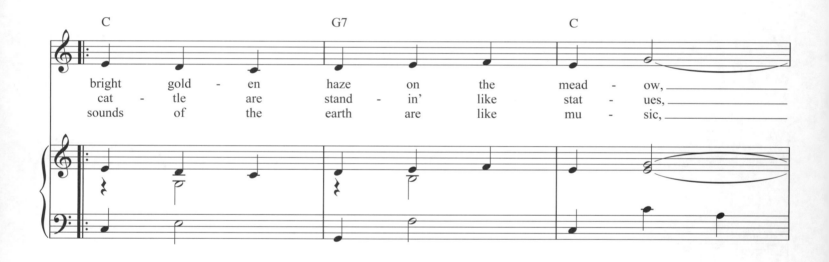

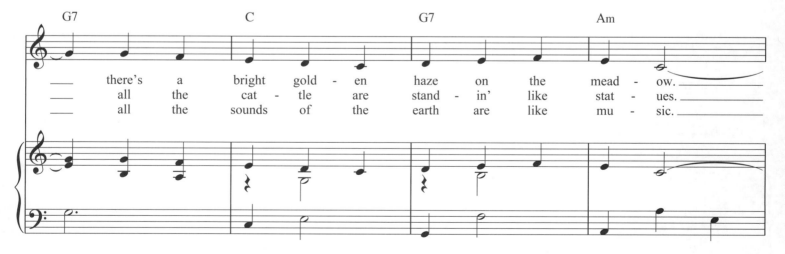

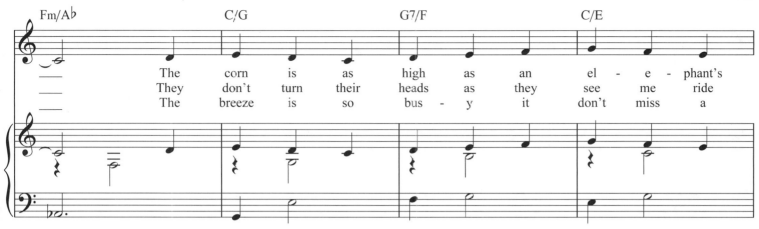

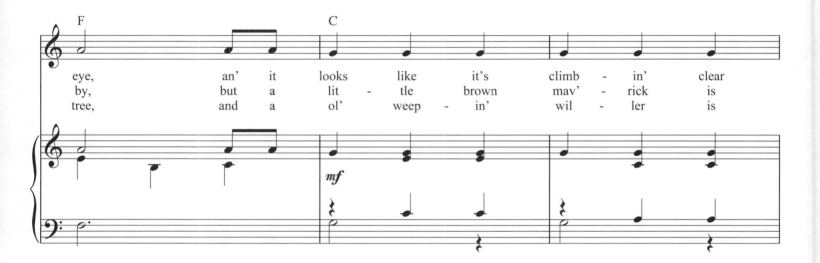

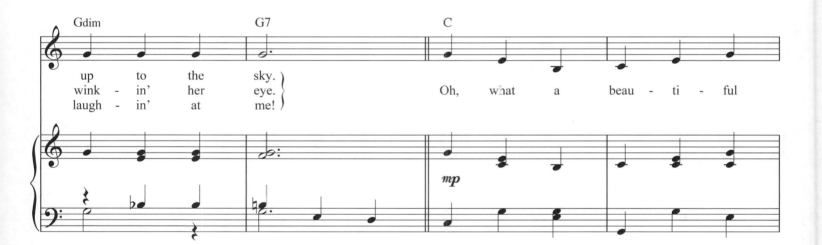

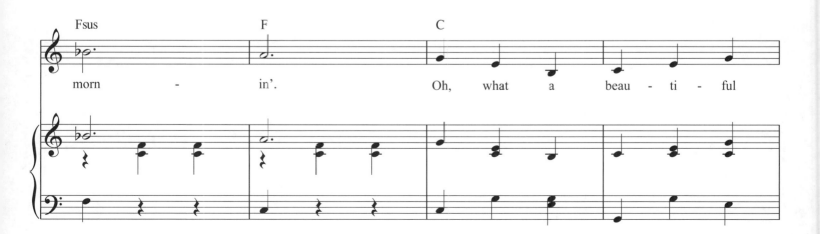

146

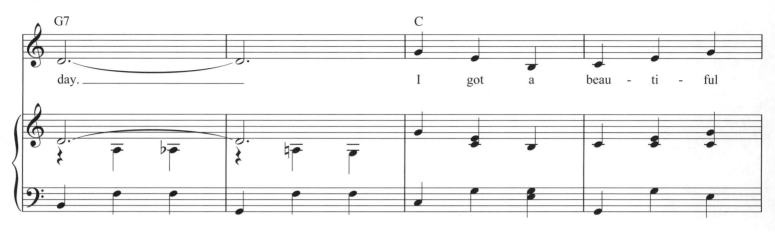

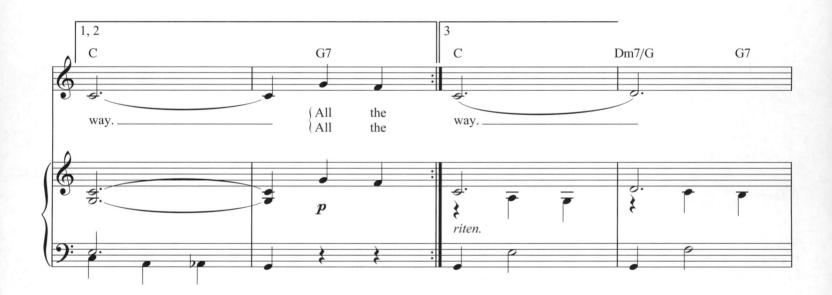

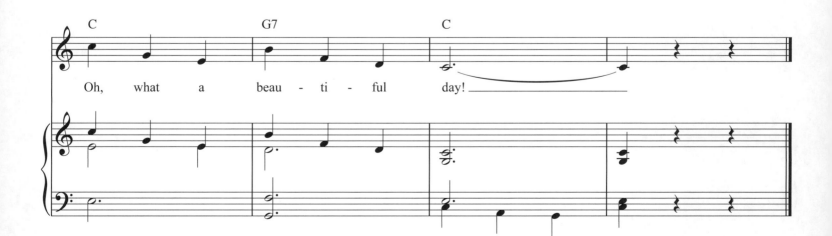

# ON THE STREET WHERE YOU LIVE

from MY FAIR LADY

Words by ALAN JAY LERNER
Music by FREDERICK LOEWE

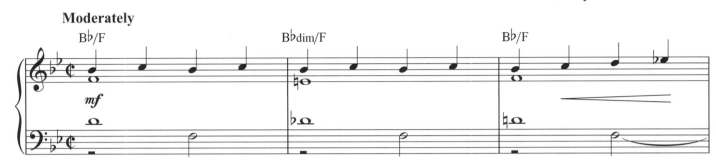

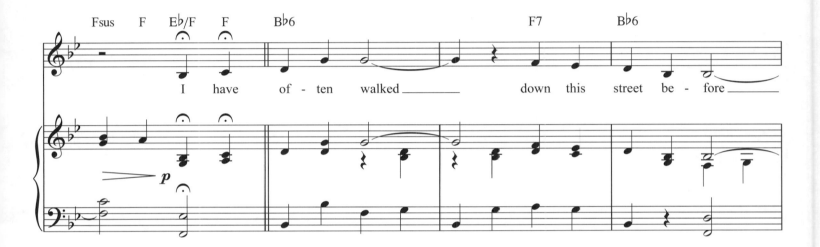

I have of-ten walked _____ down this street be - fore _____

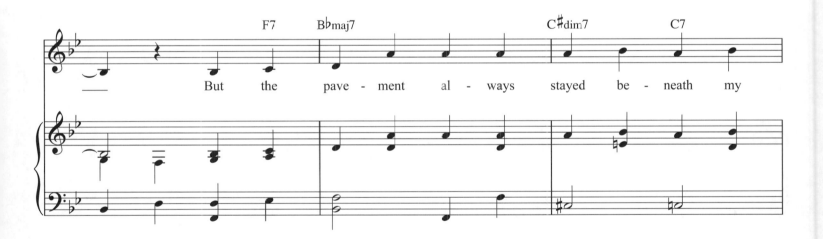

_____ But the pave-ment al - ways stayed be - neath my

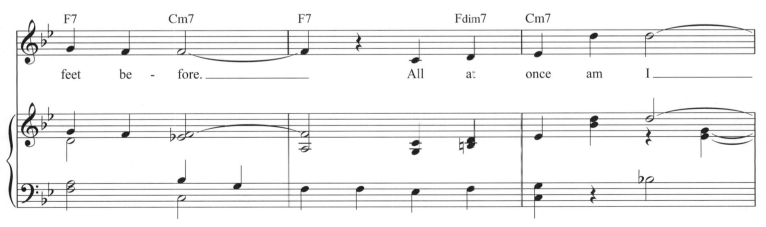

feet be - fore. _____ All at once am I _____

148

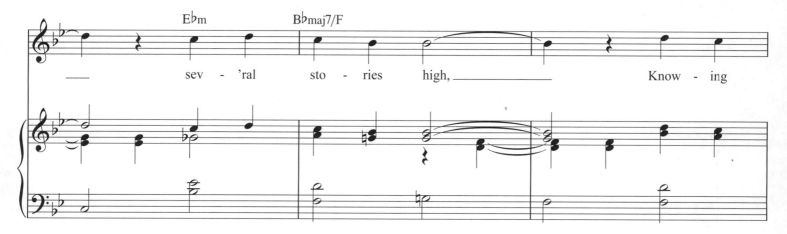

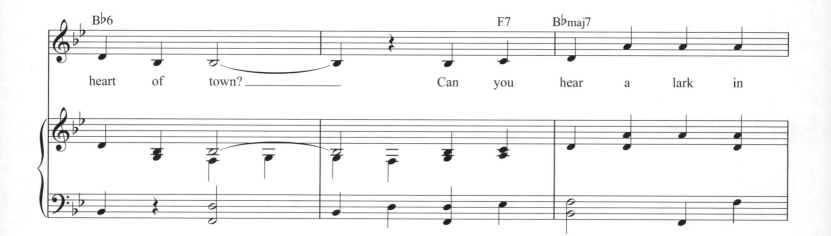

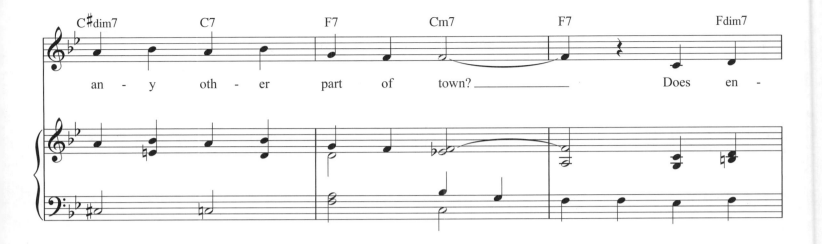

an - y oth - er part of town? _____ Does en -

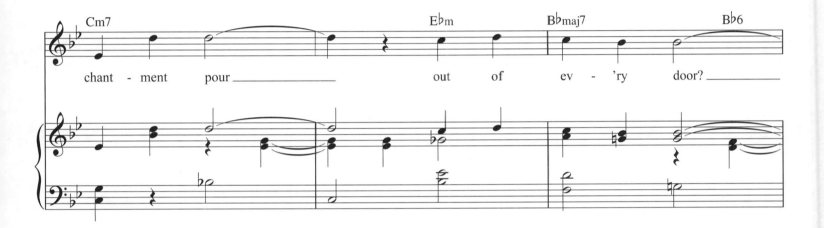

chant - ment pour _____ out of ev - 'ry door? _____

\_\_\_ No, it's just on the street where you

live. _____ And oh, _____ the tow - er - ing

feel - ing, _____ Just to know _____

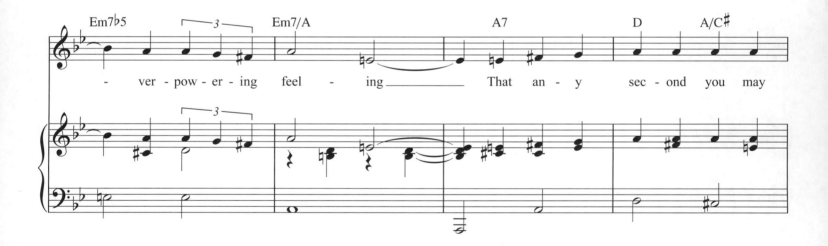

___ some - how you are near! _____ The o -

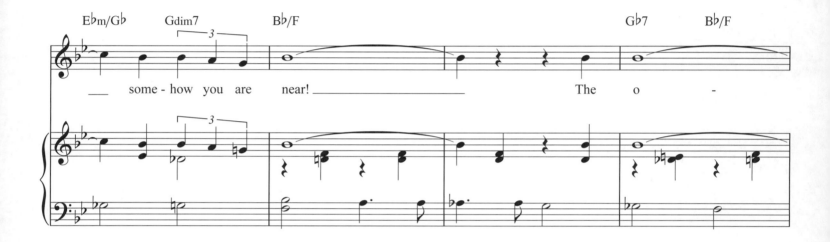

- ver - pow - er - ing feel - ing _____ That an - y sec - ond you may

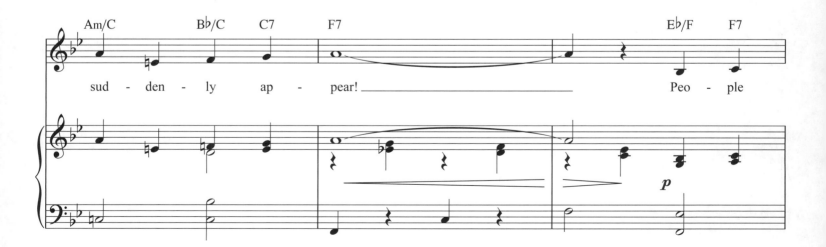

sud - den - ly ap - pear! _____ Peo - ple

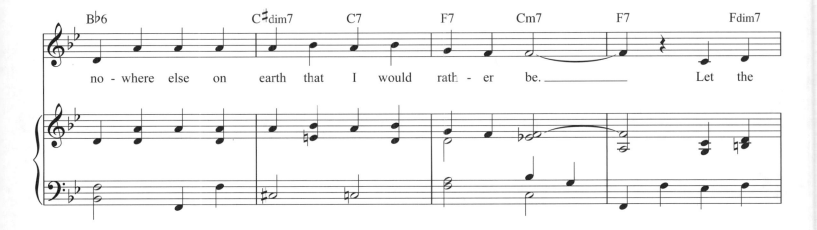

# PART OF YOUR WORLD

## from THE LITTLE MERMAID - A Broadway Musical

Music by ALAN MENKEN
Lyrics by HOWARD ASHMAN

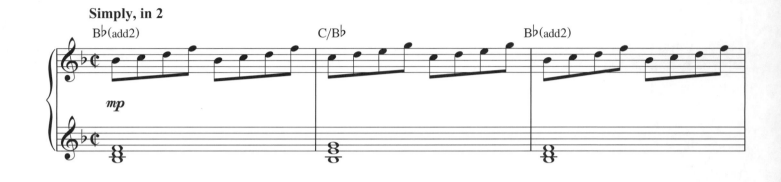

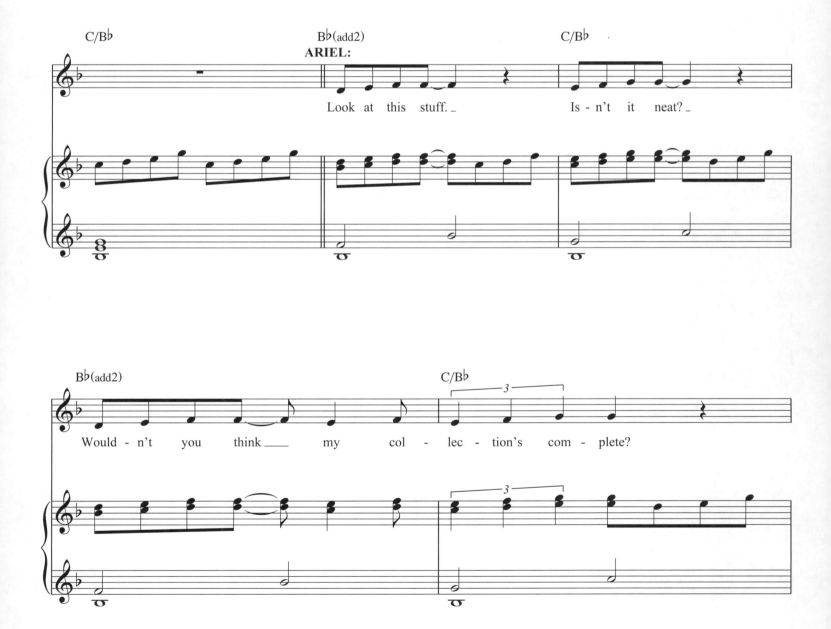

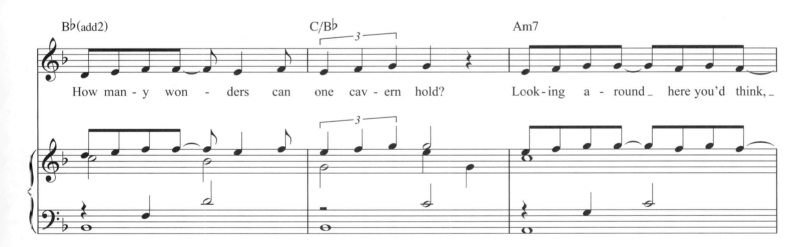

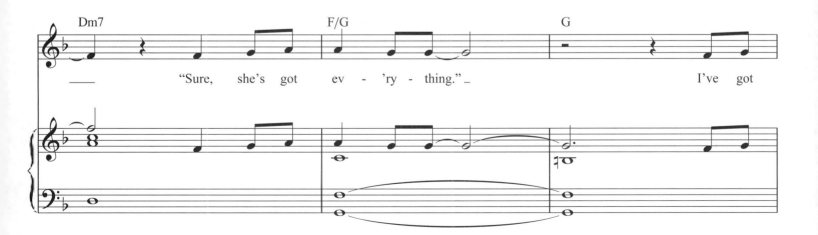

154

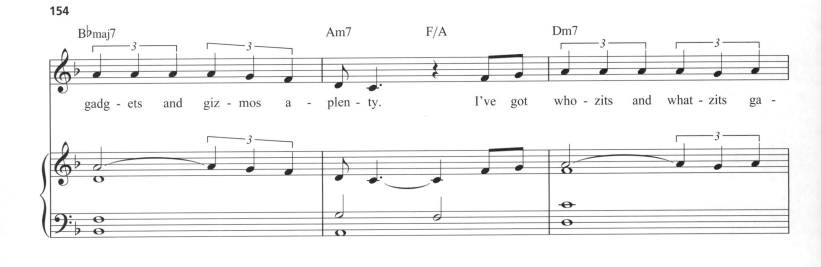

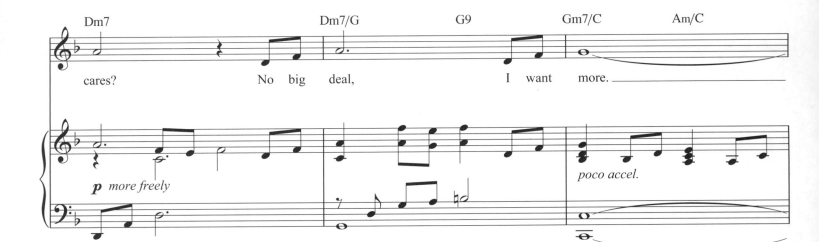

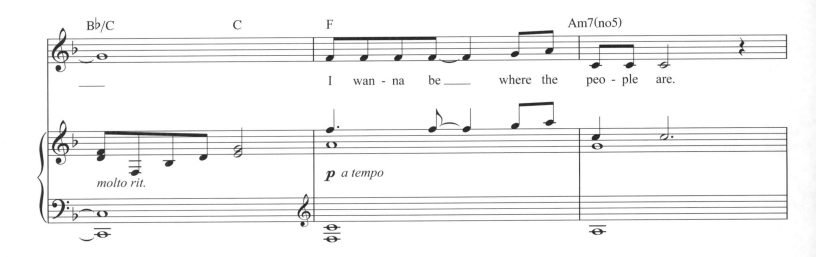

Street. Up where they walk, up where they
run, up where they stay all day in the sun. Wan - der - in'

free, wish I could be part of that world.

What would I give if I could live out - ta these

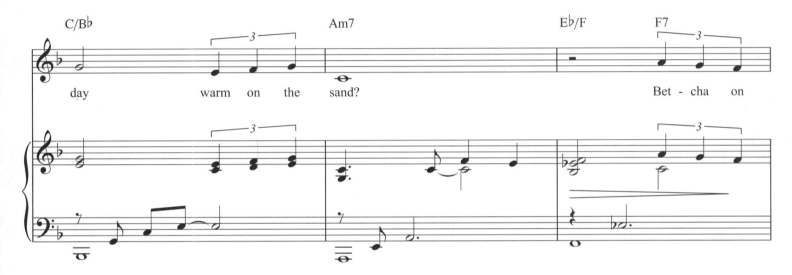

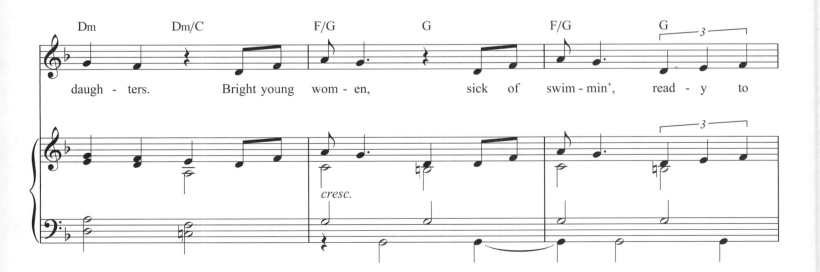

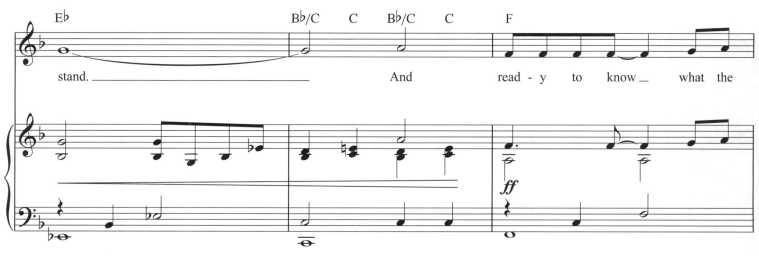

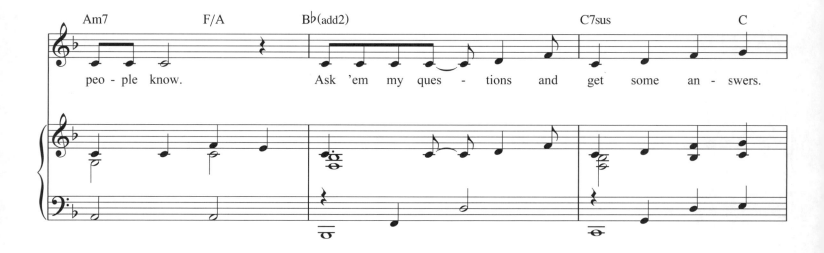

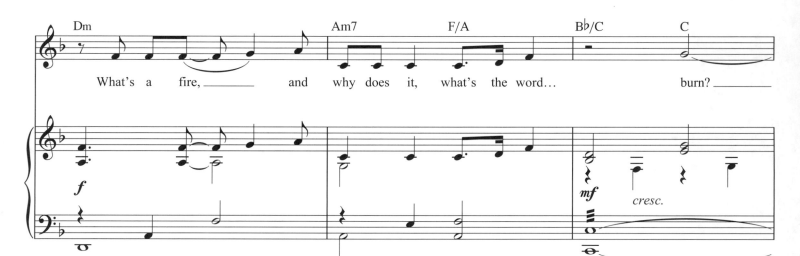

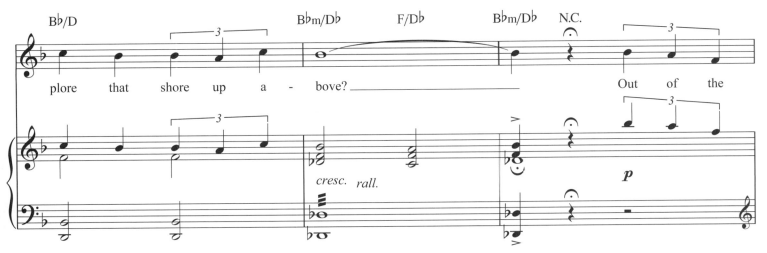

plore that shore up a - bove? _____ Out of the

**Freely**

sea, wish I could be

part of that world. _____

# PEOPLE
## from FUNNY GIRL

Words by BOB MERRILL
Music by JULE STYNE

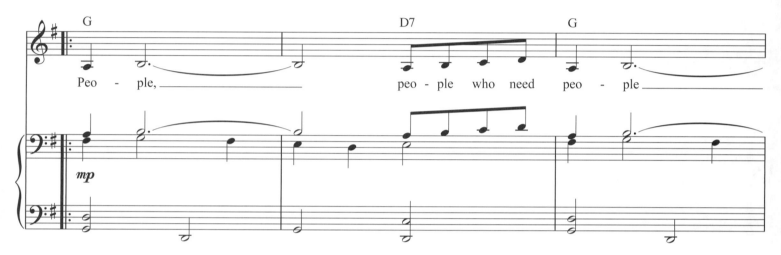

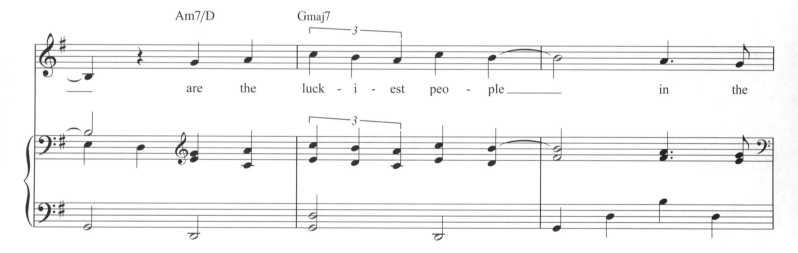

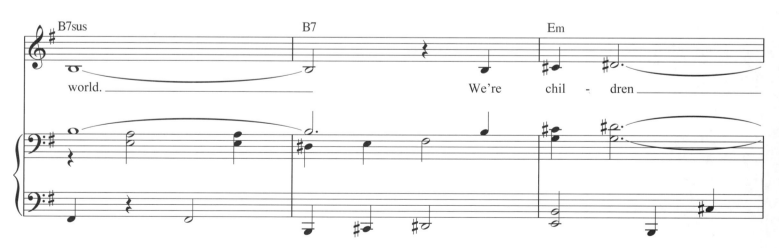

need - ing oth - er chil - dren, _____ and yet,

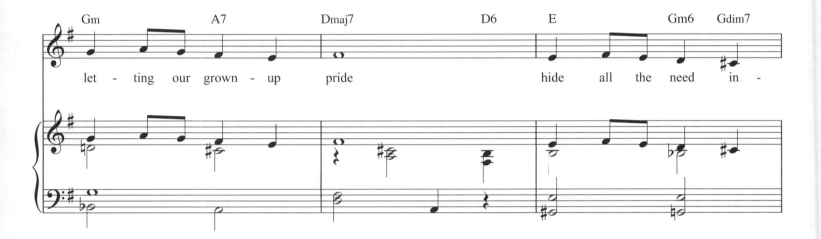

let - ting our grown - up pride hide all the need in -

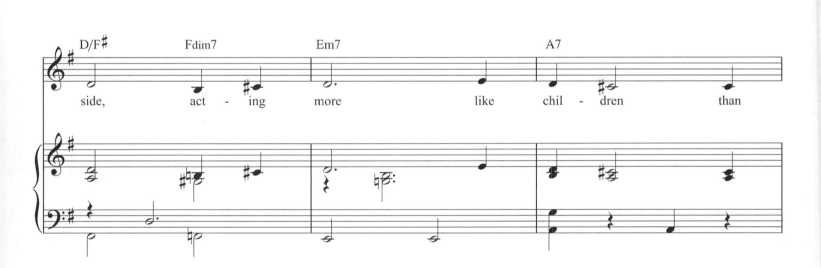

side, act - ing more like chil - dren than

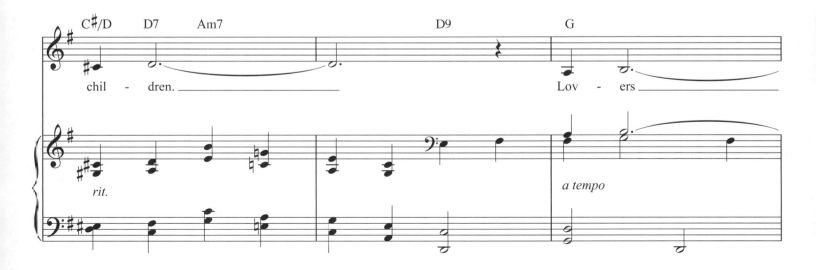

chil - dren. _____ Lov - ers _____

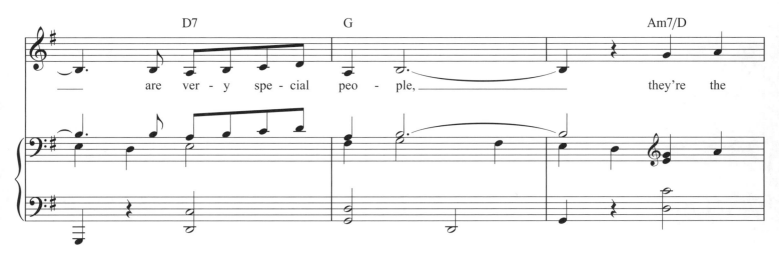

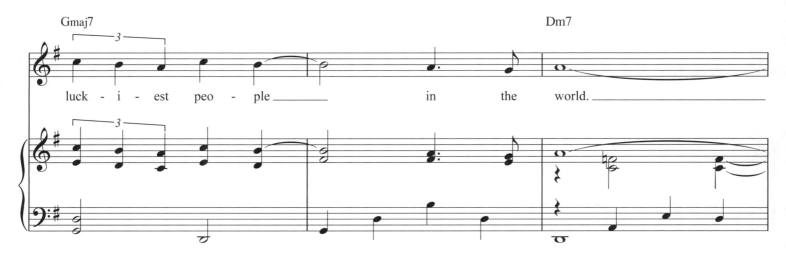

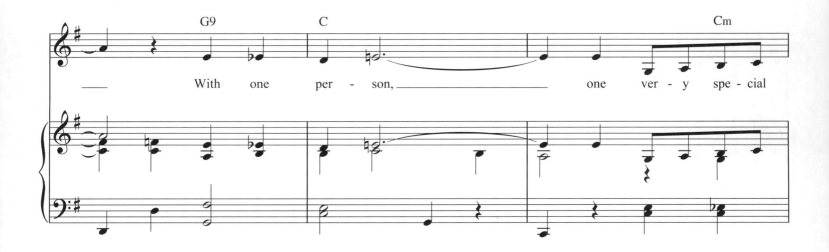

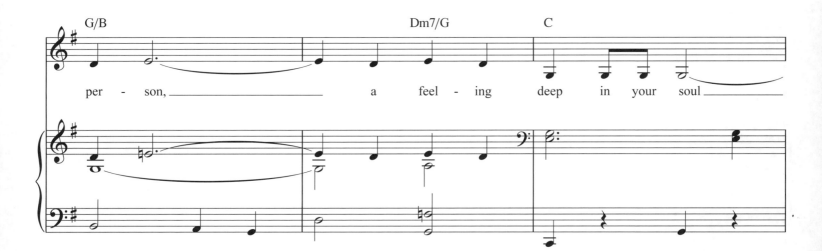

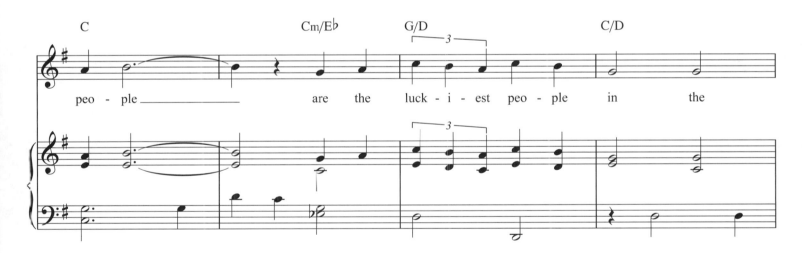

# POPULAR
## from the Broadway Musical WICKED

Music and Lyrics by
STEPHEN SCHWARTZ

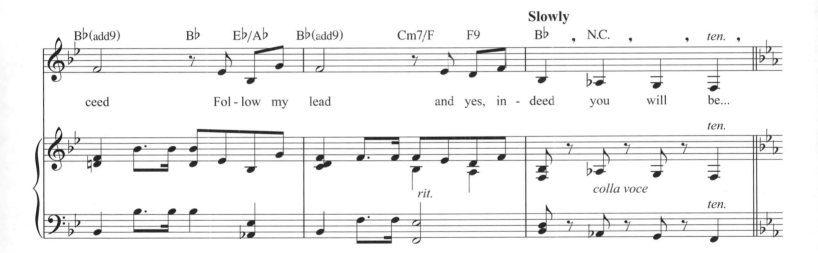

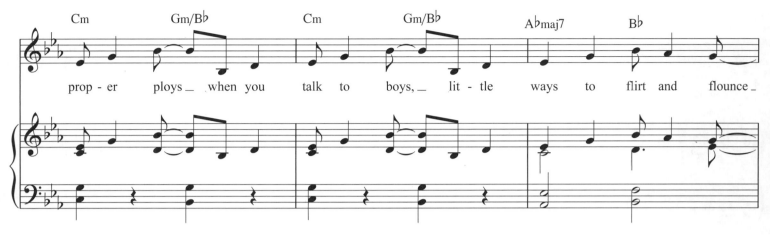

prop-er ploys __ when you talk to boys, __ lit-tle ways to flirt and flounce __

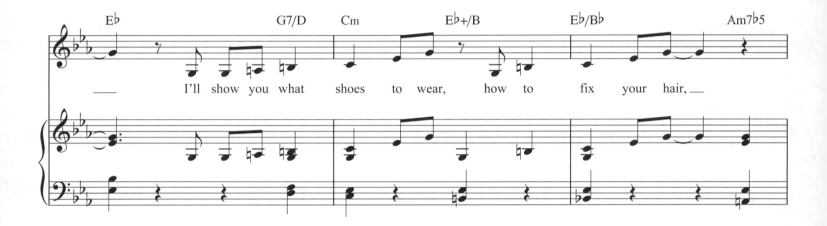

__ I'll show you what shoes to wear, how to fix your hair, __

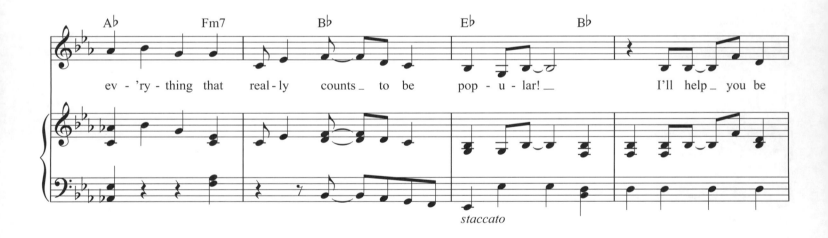

ev-'ry-thing that real-ly counts __ to be pop-u-lar! __ I'll help __ you be

*staccato*

pop-u - lar! You'll hang __ with the right co-horts, __ you'll be

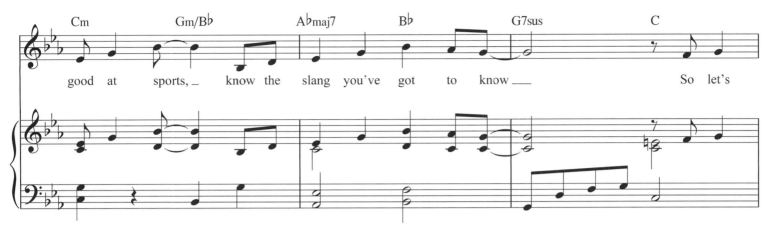

good at sports, __ know the slang you've got to know __ So let's

start, 'cause you've got an aw-f'lly long __ way to go! __

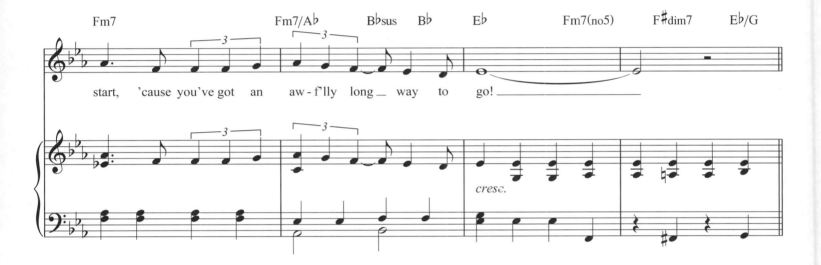

Don't be of-fend-ed by my frank an-al - y-sis Think of it as per-son-al-i-

ty di-al - y-sis Now that I've cho-sen to be-come a pal, __ a sis-

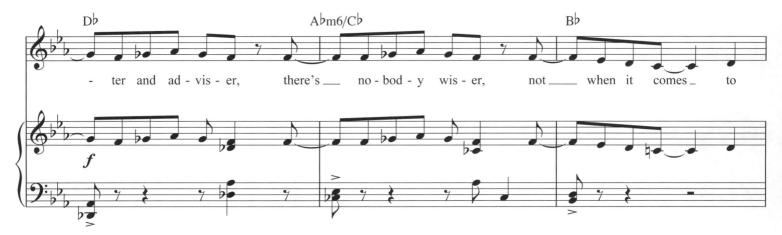

- ter and ad - vis - er, there's __ no - bod - y wis - er, not __ when it comes __ to

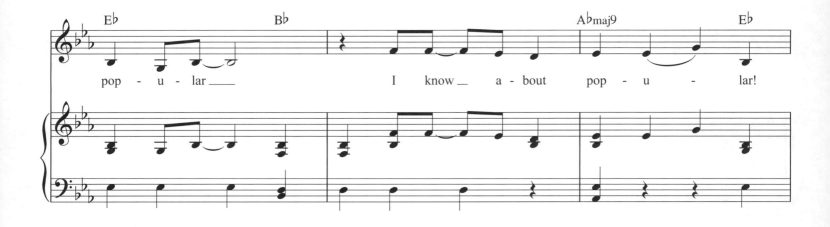

pop - u - lar __ I know __ a - bout pop - u - lar!

And with __ an as - sist from me __ to be who you'll be, __ in -

stead of drear - y who - you - were... __ are... There's noth - ing that can stop you from __

169

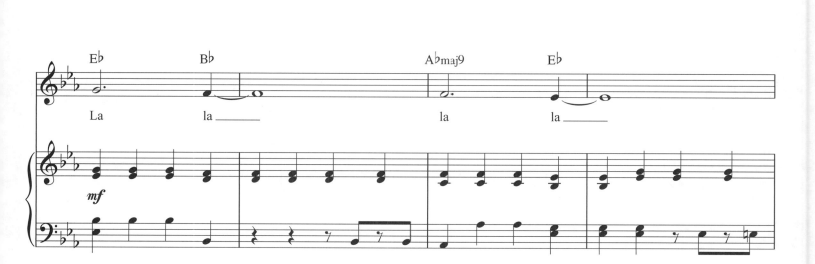

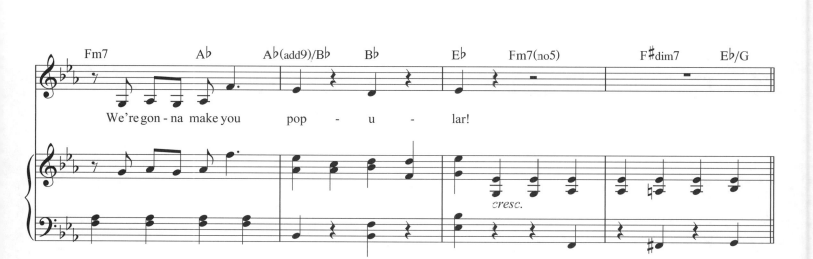

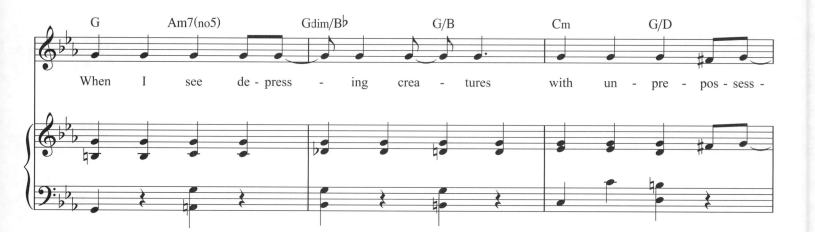

pop - u - lar! It's not ___ a - bout ap - ti - tude, ___ it's the

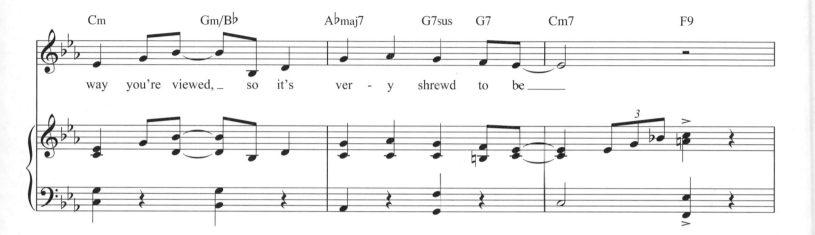

way you're viewed, ___ so it's ver - y shrewd to be ___

ver - y, ver - y pop - u - lar like me! And tho'

**Freely**

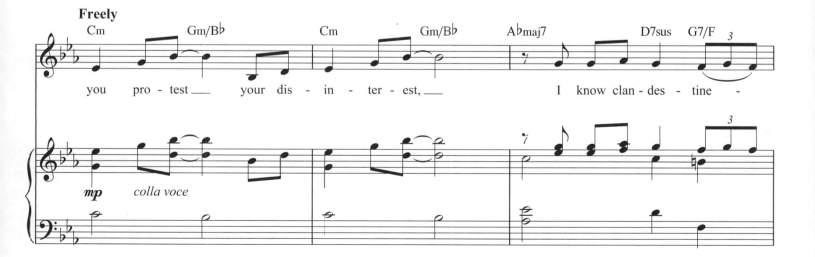

you pro - test ___ your dis - in - ter - est, ___ I know clan - des - tine -

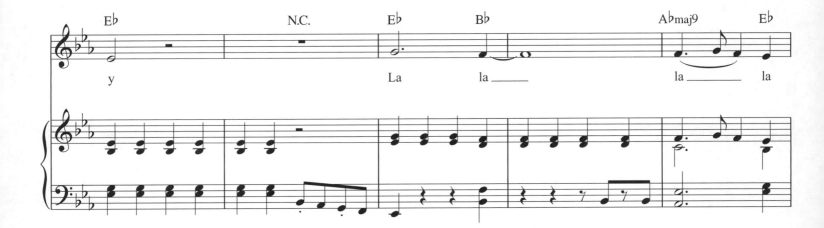

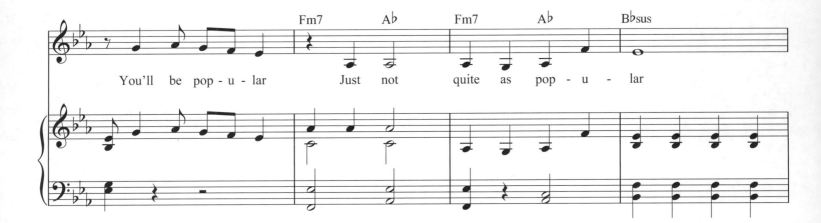

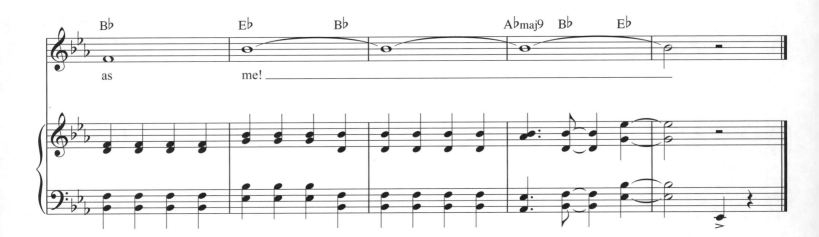

# PUT ON A HAPPY FACE
## from BYE BYE BIRDIE

Lyric by LEE ADAMS
Music by CHARLES STROUSE

**Rhythmically, lightly**

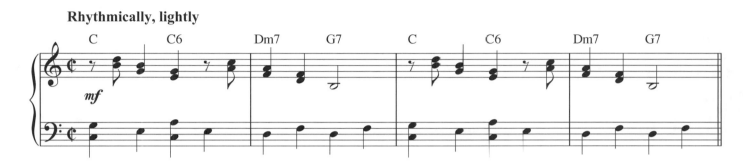

Gray skies are gon - na clear up, _____ put on a hap - py

face; Brush off the clouds and cheer up, _____

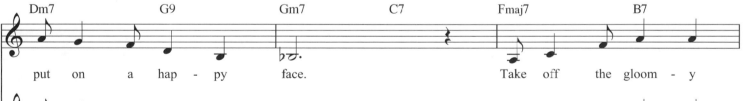

put on a hap - py face. Take off the gloom - y

mask of trag - e - dy, it's not your style;

You'll look so good that you'll be glad ___ ya' de - cid - ed to smile! ___

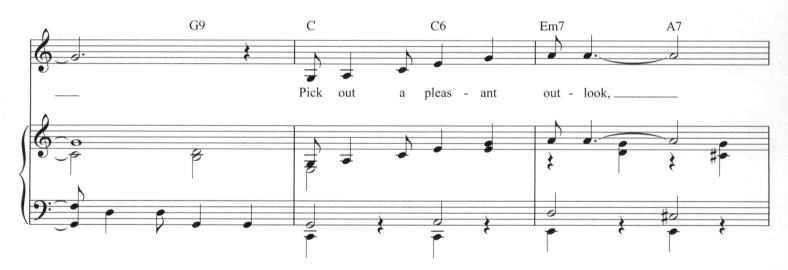

___ Pick out a pleas - ant out - look, ___

stick out that no - ble chin; Wipe off that "full of

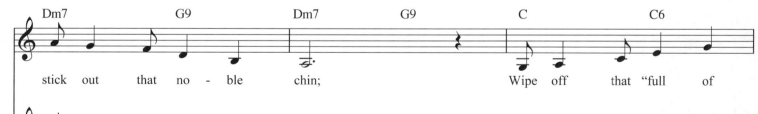

doubt" look, _____ slap on a hap - py grin! And

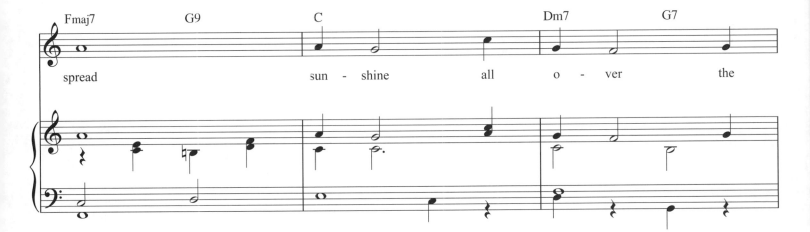

spread sun - shine all o - ver the

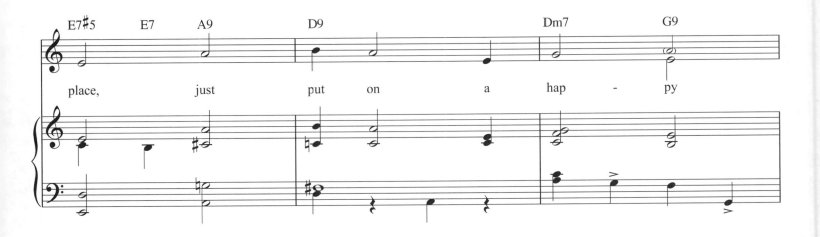

place, just put on a hap - py

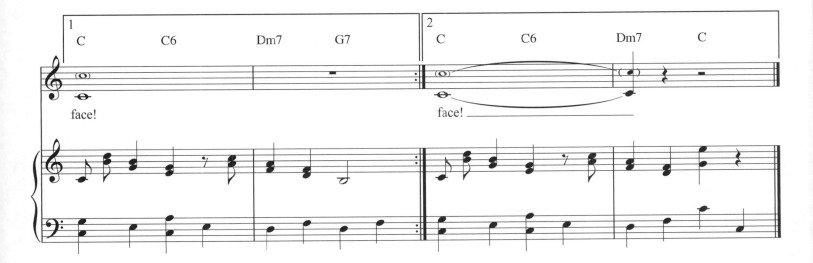

face!          face! _____

# SEND IN THE CLOWNS
### from the Musical A LITTLE NIGHT MUSIC

Words and Music by
STEPHEN SONDHEIM

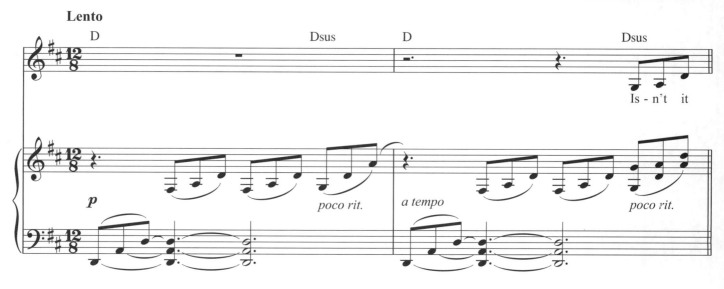

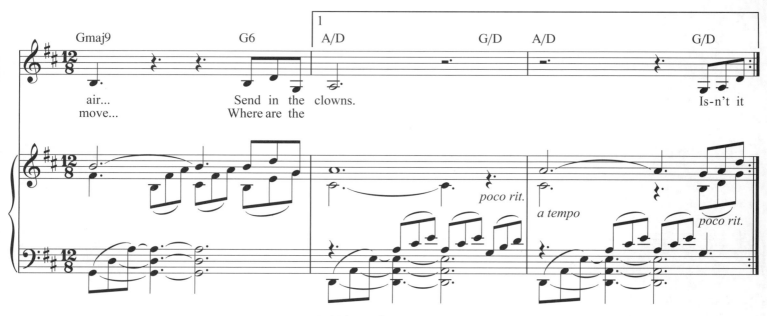

177

# SOME ENCHANTED EVENING

## from SOUTH PACIFIC

Lyrics by OSCAR HAMMERSTEIN II
Music by RICHARD RODGERS

**Moderato**

*slowly, with expression*

Some en-chant-ed eve-ning ____ you may see a stran-ger, ____

____ you may see a stran-ger ____ a-cross a

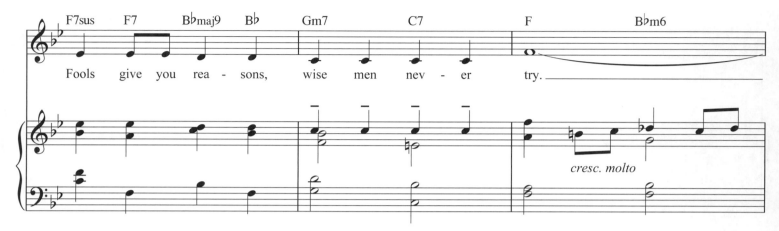

Fools give you rea - sons, wise men nev - er try. ___

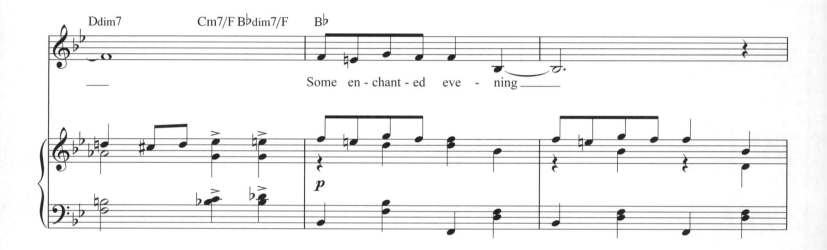

___ Some en - chant - ed eve - ning ___

when you find your true love, ___ when you feel her call you ___

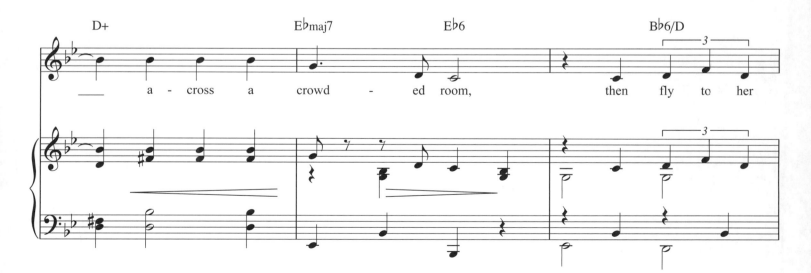

___ a - cross a crowd - ed room, then fly to her

# SHY
## from ONCE UPON A MATTRESS

Words by MARSHALL BARER
Music by MARY RODGERS

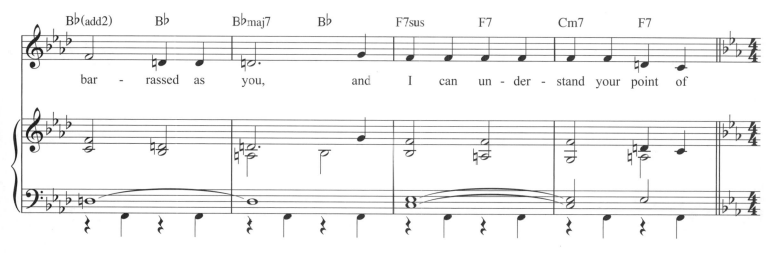

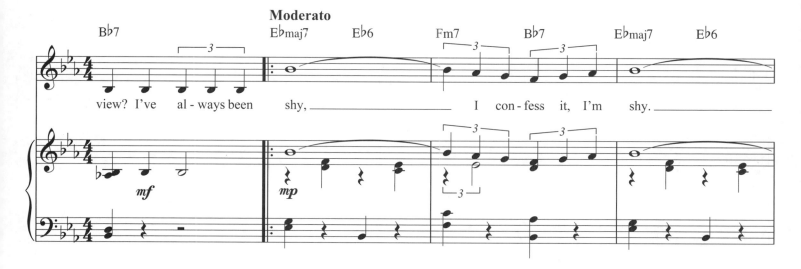

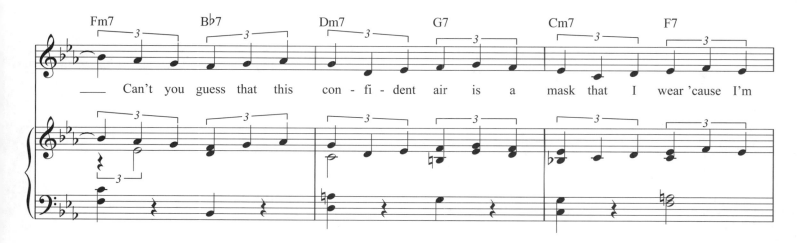

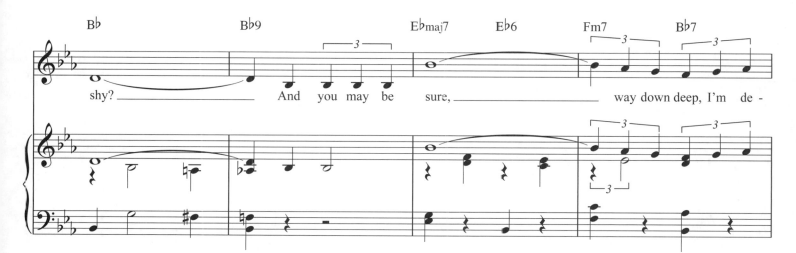

mure._____ Though some peo - ple I know might de - ny it, at

bot - tom I'm qui - et and pure._____ I'm a - ware that it's wrong_____ to be

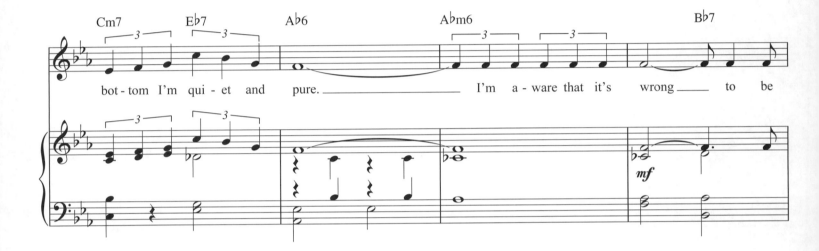

meek as I am; my chanc - es may pass me by. I pre - tend to be

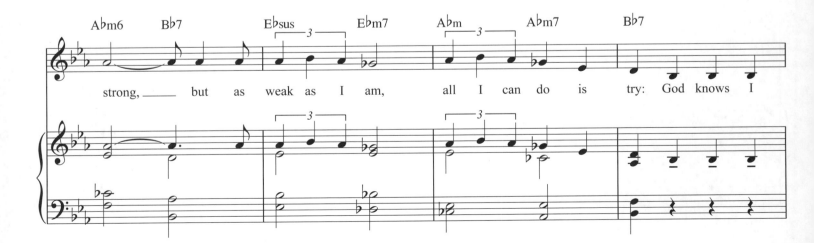

strong,_____ but as weak as I am, all I can do is try: God knows I

try, _____ though I'm fright-ened and shy; _____

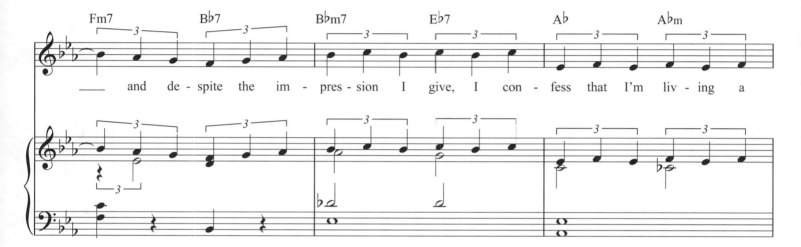

____ and de-spite the im-pres-sion I give, I con-fess that I'm liv-ing a

lie! _____ Be-cause I'm ac-tual-ly ter-ri-bly tim-id and hor-rib-ly

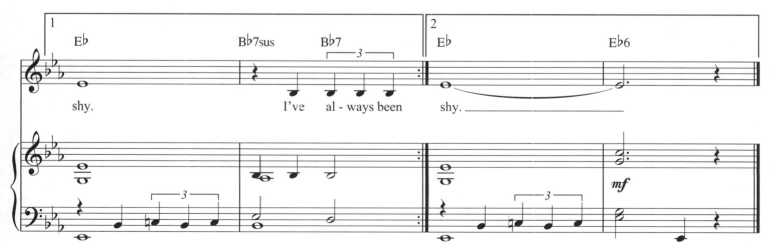

shy.

I've al-ways been shy. _____

# SOMEONE TO WATCH OVER ME

## from OH, KAY!

Music and Lyrics by GEORGE GERSHWIN
and IRA GERSHWIN

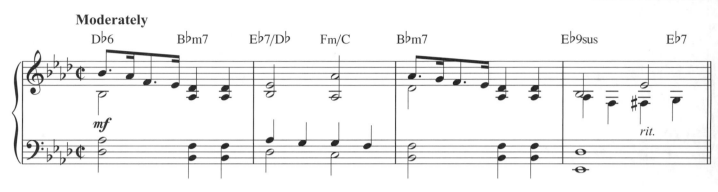

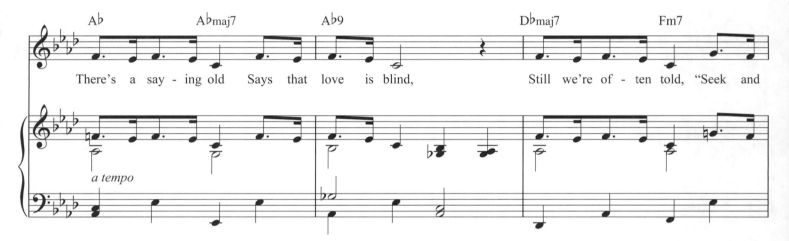

There's a say - ing old Says that love is blind, Still we're of - ten told, "Seek and

ye shall find." So I'm going to seek A cer - tain lad I've

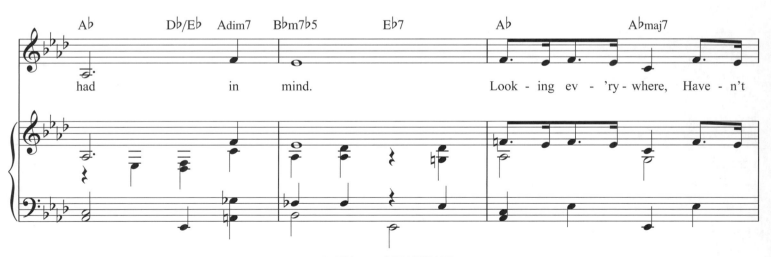

had in mind. Look - ing ev - 'ry - where, Have - n't

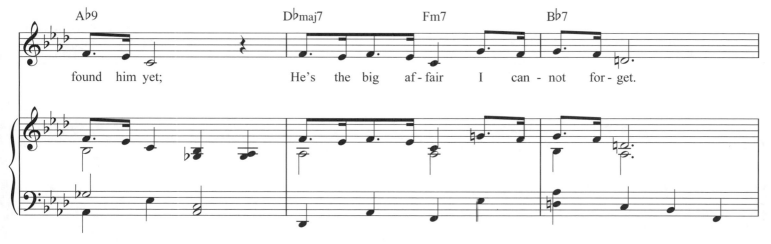

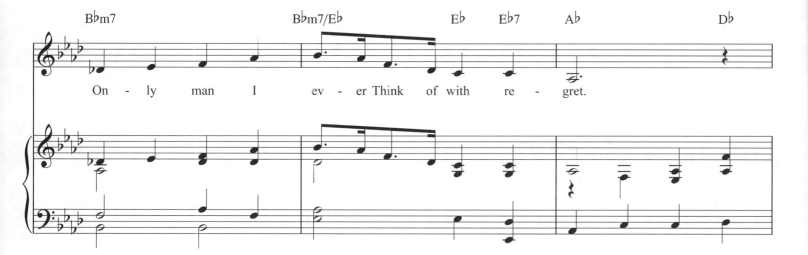

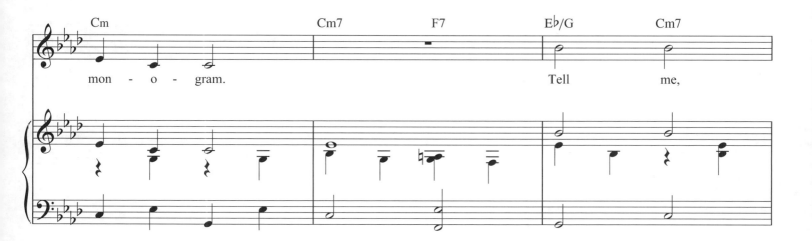

190

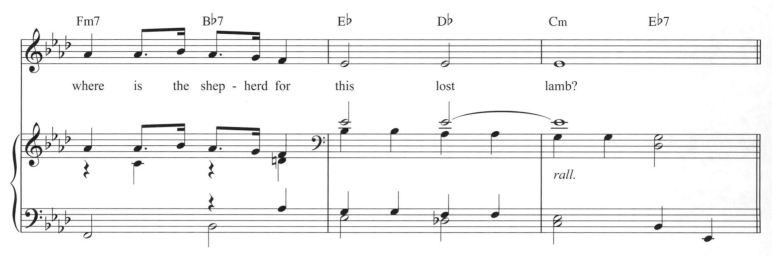

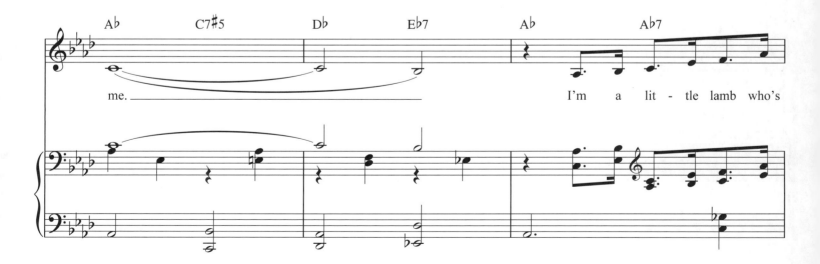

lost in the wood. I know I could Al - ways be good

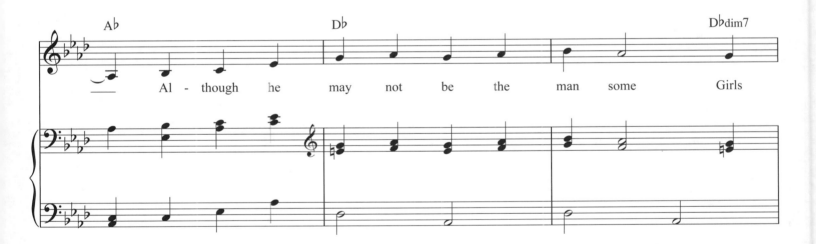

To one who'll watch o - ver me. _____

Al - though he may not be the man some Girls

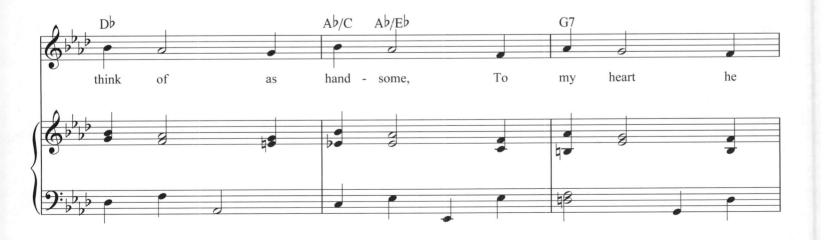

think of as hand - some, To my heart he

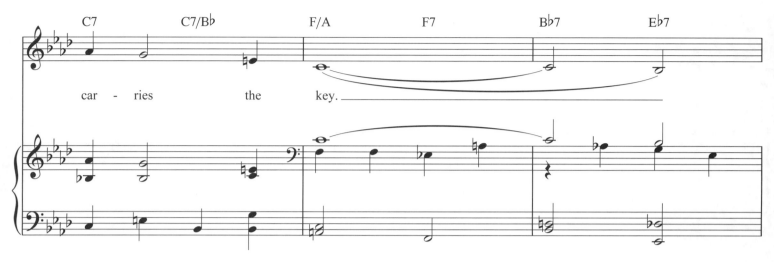

car - ries the key.

Won't you tell him please to put on some speed, Fol - low my lead,

Oh, how I need Some - one to watch o - ver

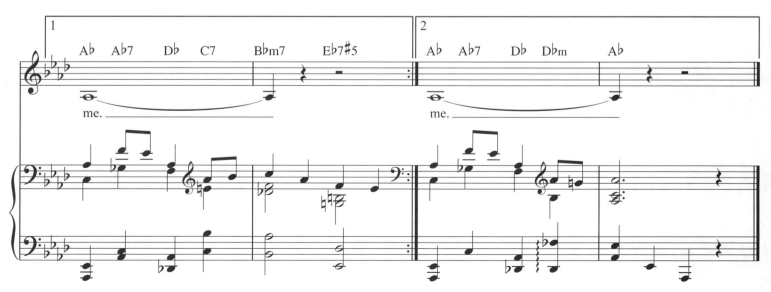

me.

me.

# THE SOUND OF MUSIC
## from THE SOUND OF MUSIC

Lyrics by OSCAR HAMMERSTEIN II
Music by RICHARD RODGERS

Molto moderato *(tenderly)*

194

**Refrain** *(moderately, with warm expression)*

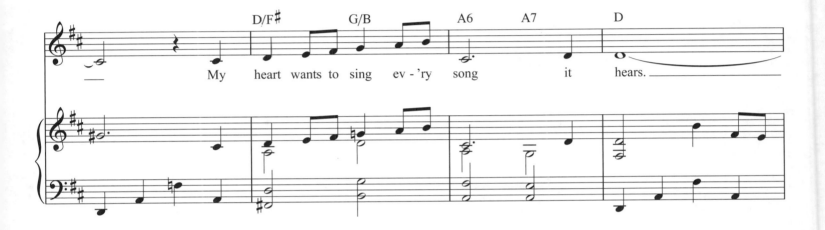

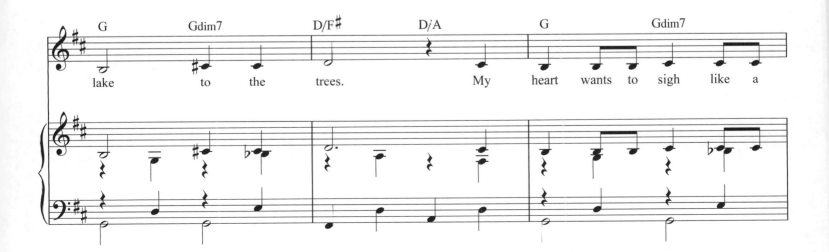

chime that flies from a church on a breeze, To laugh like a brook when it

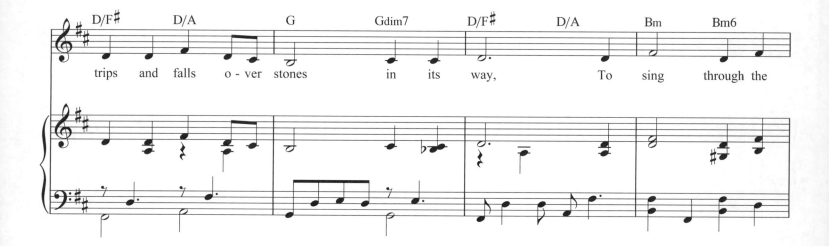

trips and falls o - ver stones in its way, To sing through the

night like a lark who is learn - ing to pray. I

go to the hills when my heart is lone - ly. I

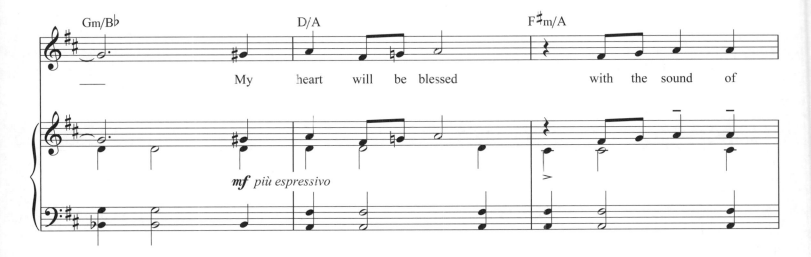

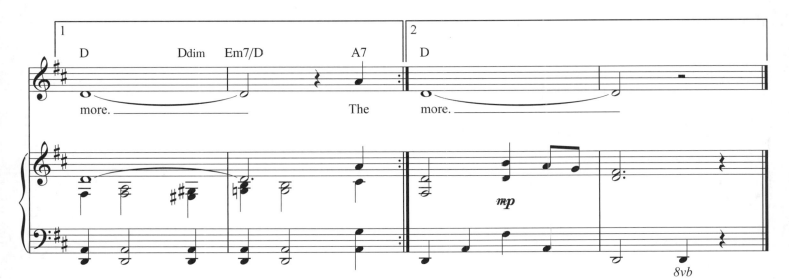

# THERE'S NO BUSINESS LIKE SHOW BUSINESS

from the Stage Production ANNIE GET YOUR GUN

Words and Music by
IRVING BERLIN

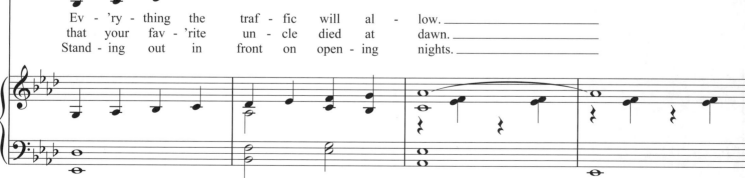

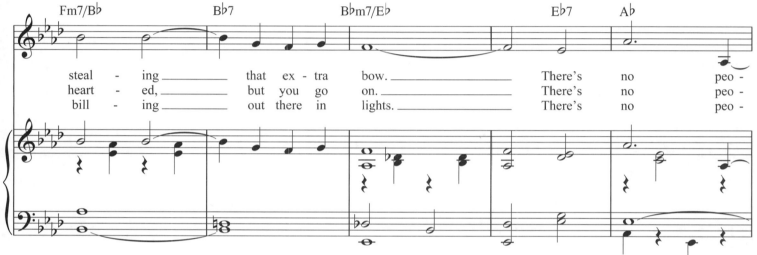

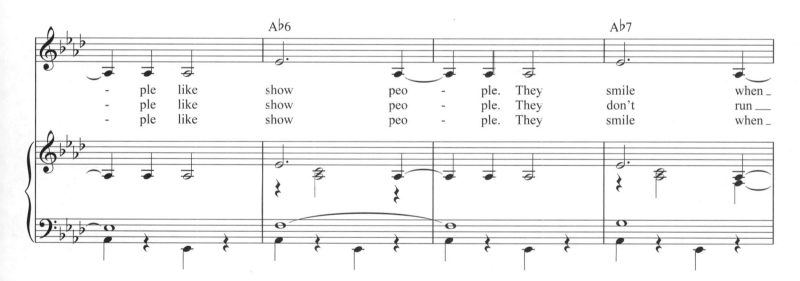

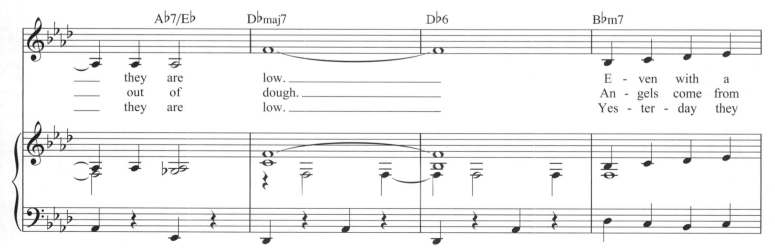

turkey that you know will fold,_____ you may be strand-
ev-'ry-where with lots of jack._____ And when you lose_____
told you you would not go far._____ That night you o-

-ed out in the cold._____ Still you would-n't
it, there's no at-tack._____ Where could you get
-pen and there you are._____ Next day on your

change it for a sack of gold._____ ⎫ Let's go on_____
mon-ey that you don't give back._____ ⎬
dress-ing room they've hung a star._____ ⎭

_____ with the show._____ There's show._____

# TILL THERE WAS YOU

## from Meredith Willson's THE MUSIC MAN

By MEREDITH WILLSON

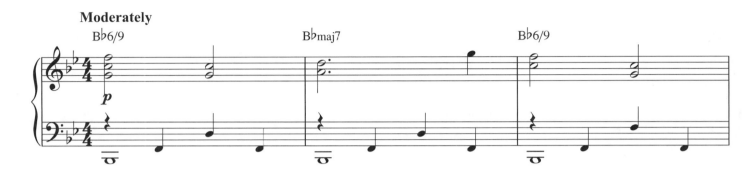

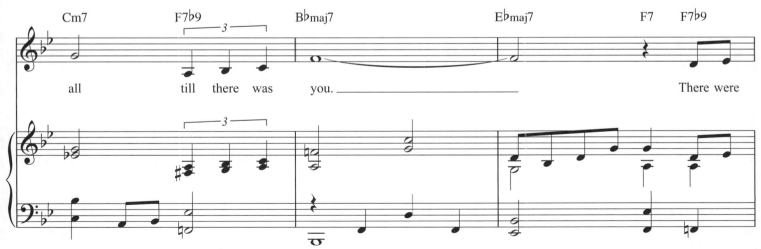

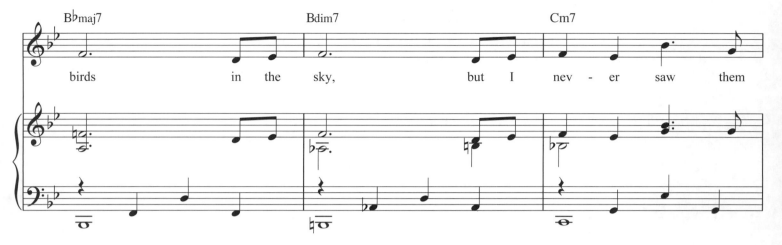

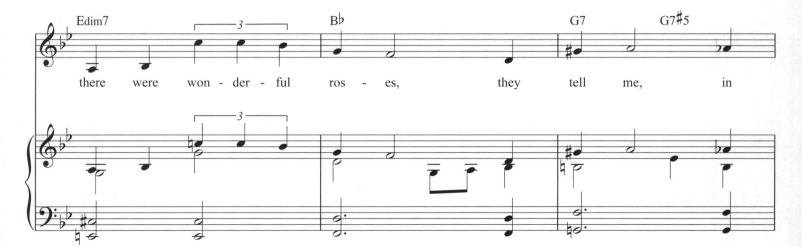

# TOMORROW
## from the Musical Production ANNIE

Lyric by MARTIN CHARNIN
Music by CHARLES STROUSE

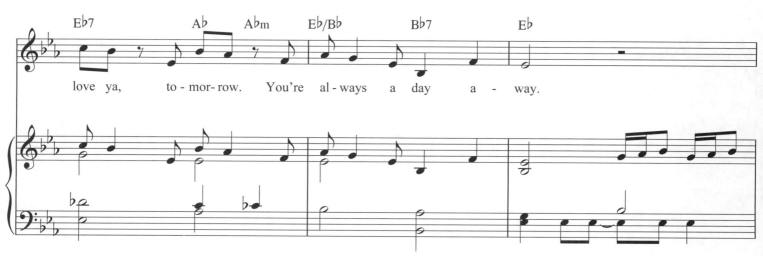

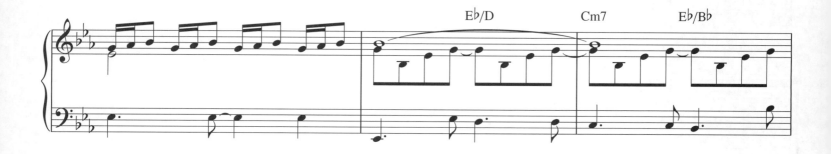

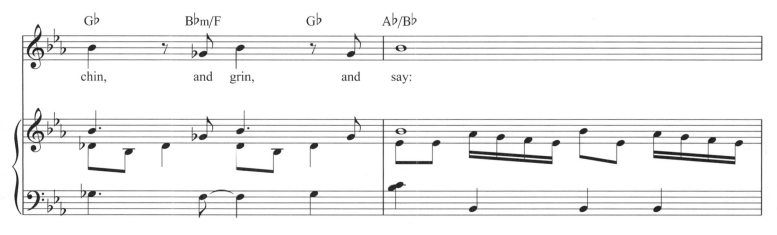

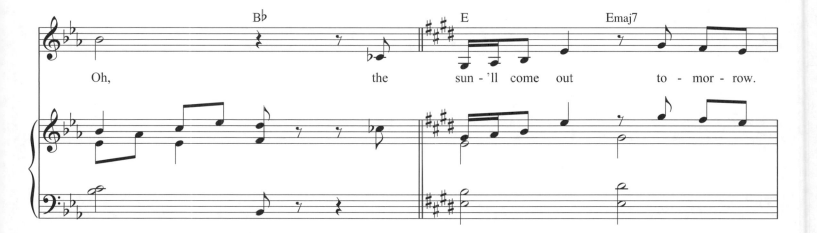

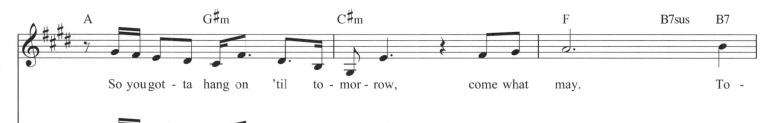

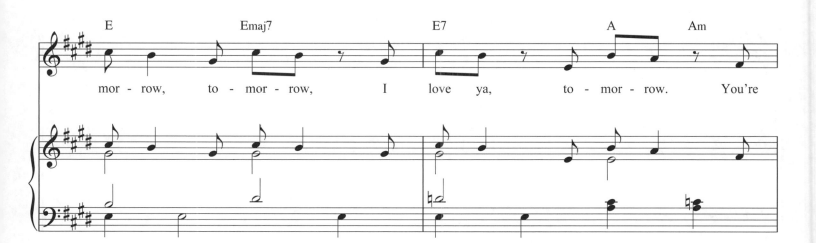

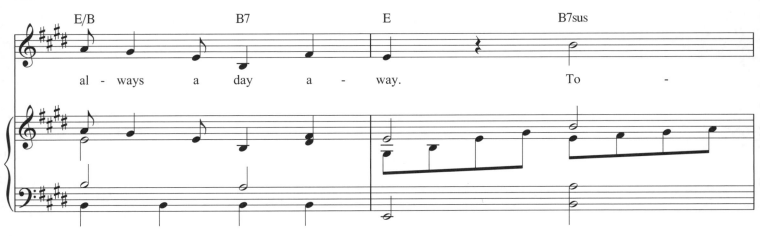

al - ways a day a - way. To -

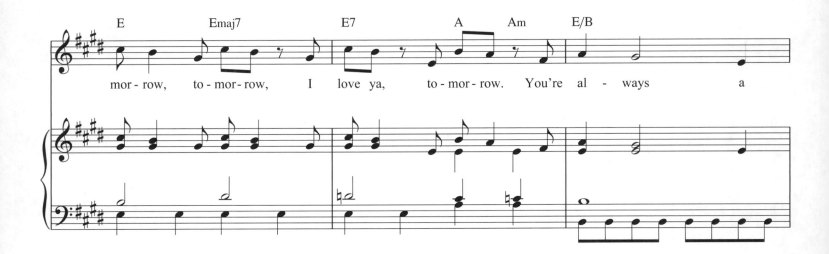

mor - row, to - mor - row, I love ya, to - mor - row. You're al - ways a

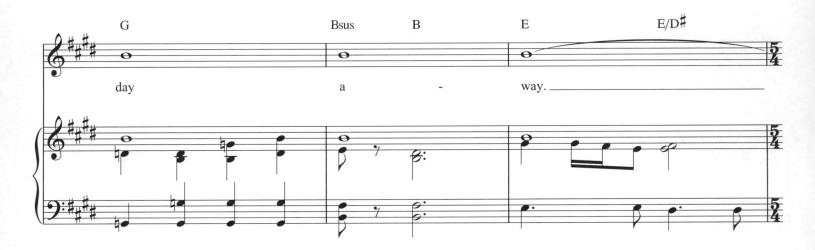

day a - way.

rit.

# TONIGHT
## from WEST SIDE STORY

Lyrics by STEPHEN SONDHEIM
Music by LEONARD BERNSTEIN

Moderate Beguine tempo

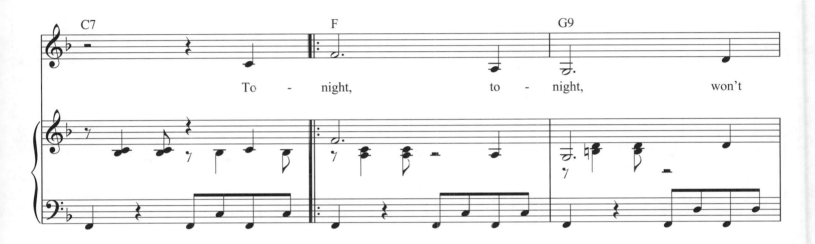

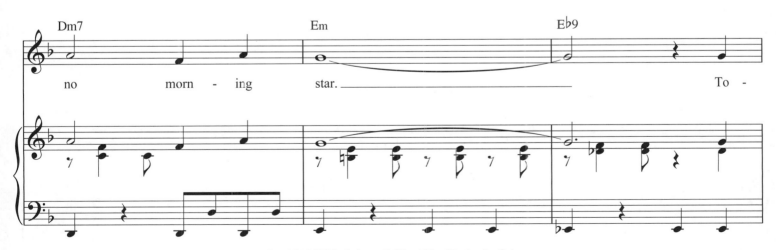

night, to - night, I'll see my love to -

night. And for us stars will stop where they

are! _____ To - day the min - utes seem like

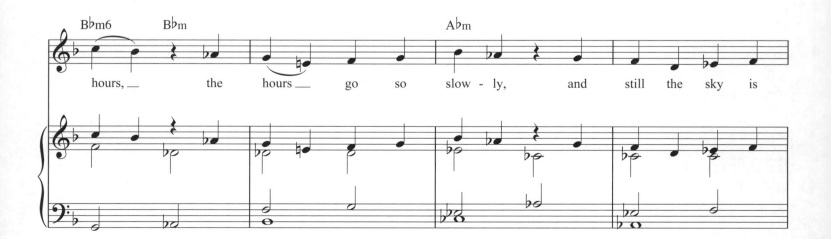

hours, __ the hours __ go so slow - ly, and still the sky is

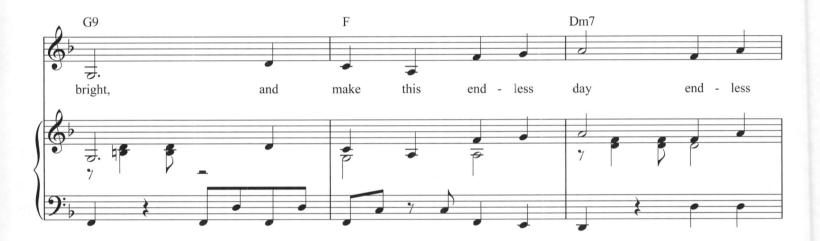

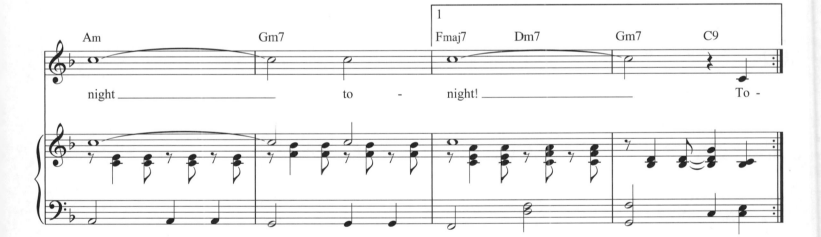

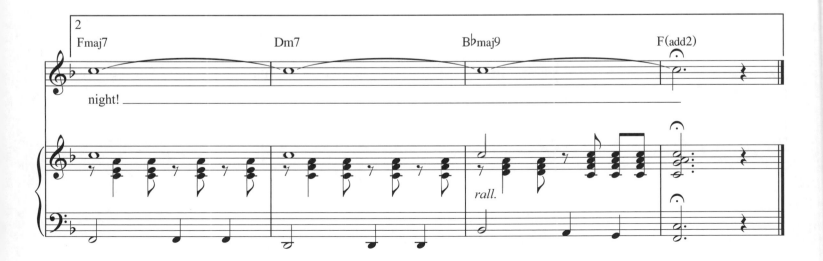

# TRY TO REMEMBER

## from THE FANTASTICKS

Words by TOM JONES
Music by HARVEY SCHMIDT

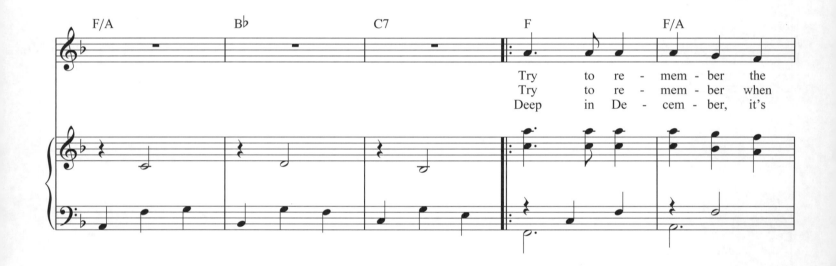

Try to re - mem - ber the
Try to re - mem - ber when
Deep in De - cem - ber, it's

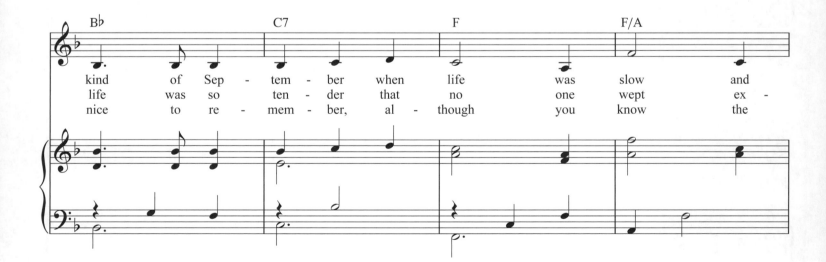

kind of Sep - tem - ber when life was slow and
life was so ten - der that no one wept ex -
nice to re - mem - ber, al - though you know the

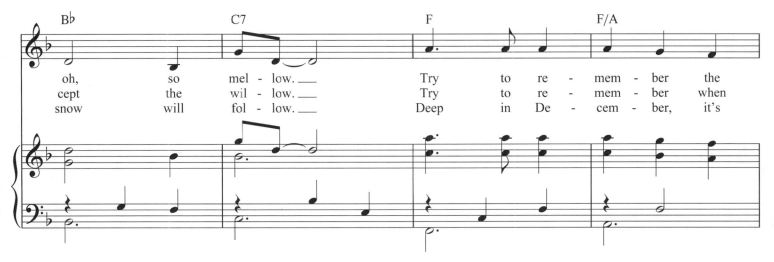

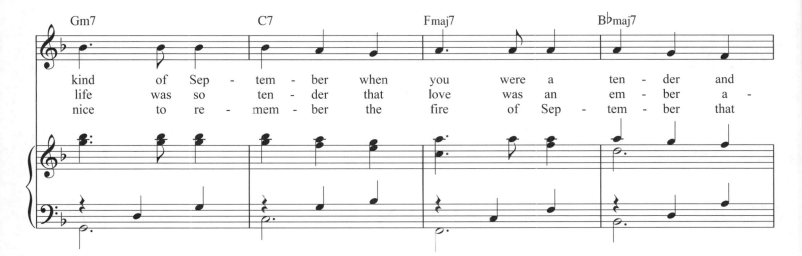

# WHERE IS LOVE?
### from the Broadway Musical OLIVER!

Words and Music by
LIONEL BART

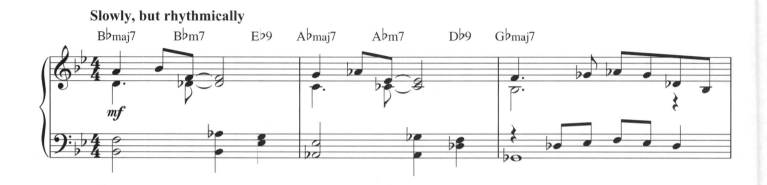

Where _____ is love?

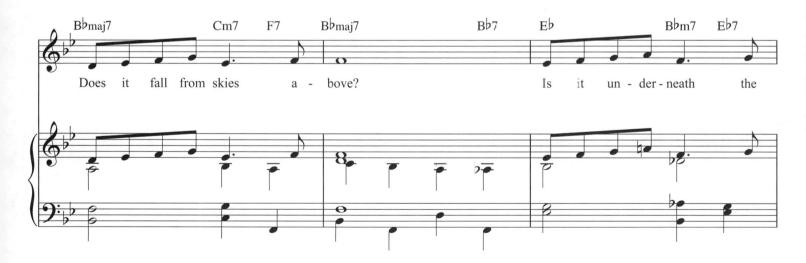

Does it fall from skies a - bove? Is it un - der - neath the

wil - low tree ___ that I've been dream - ing of?

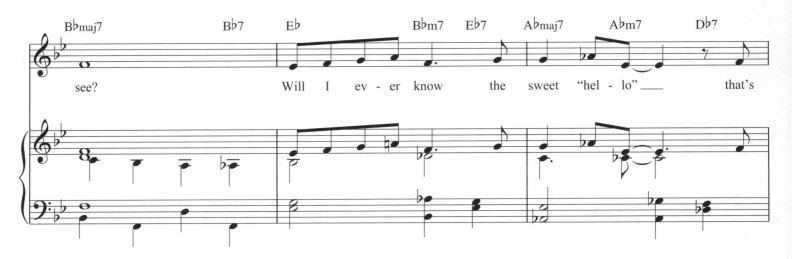

Where ___ is she who I close my eyes to

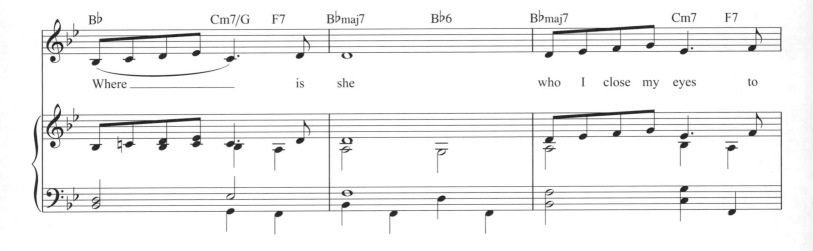

see? Will I ev - er know the sweet "hel - lo" ___ that's

meant for on - ly me? Who can say where she may
Ev - 'ry night I kneel and

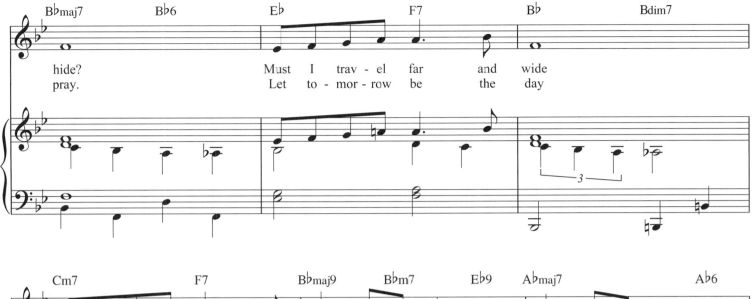

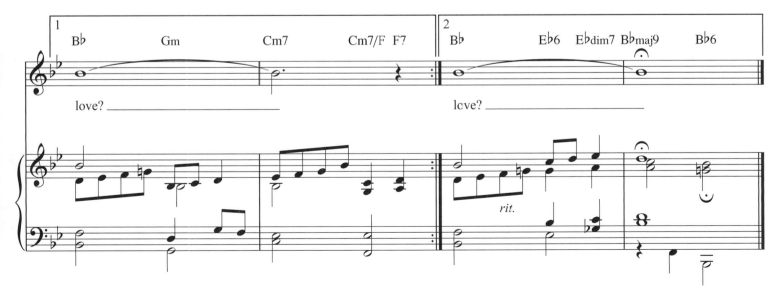

# WHAT I DID FOR LOVE

## from A CHORUS LINE

Music by MARVIN HAMLISCH
Lyric by EDWARD KLEBAN

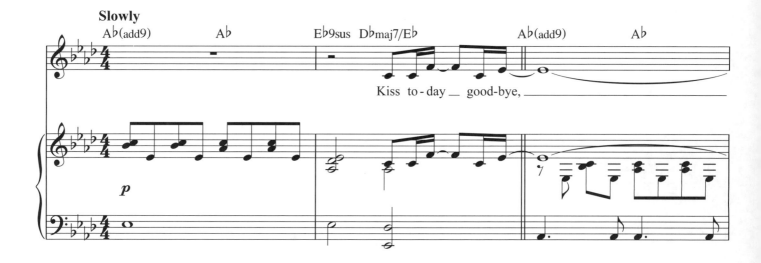

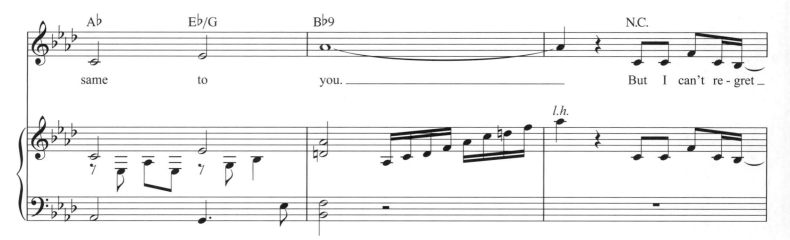

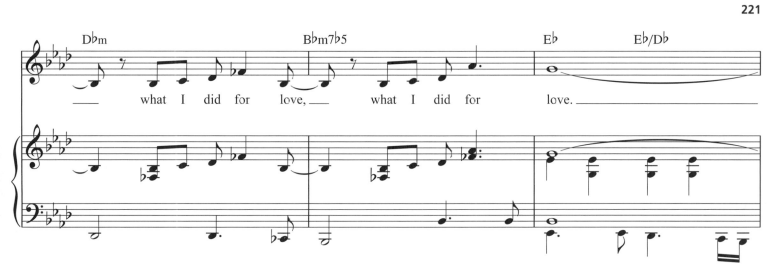

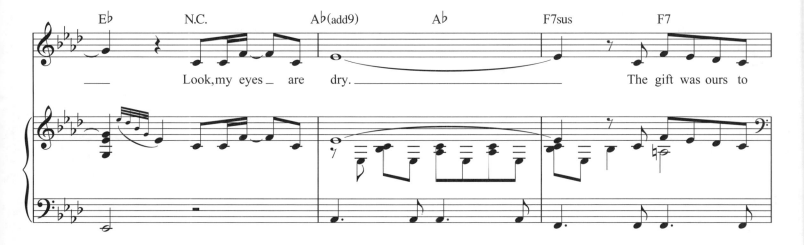

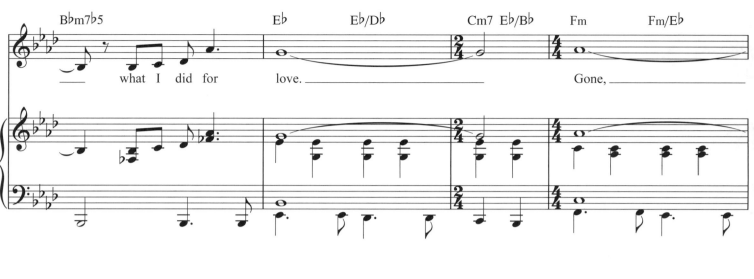

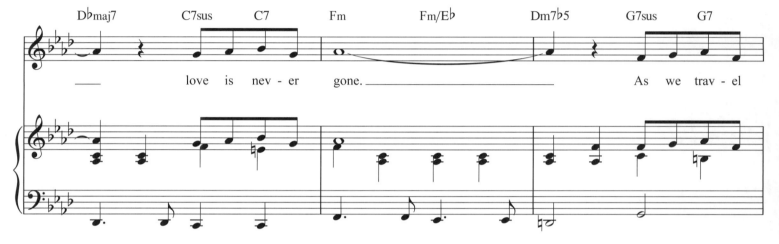

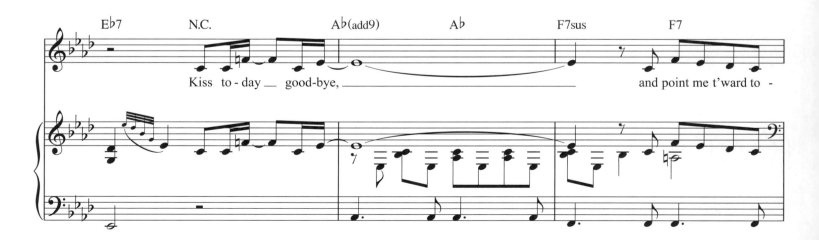

mor - row. _____ We did what _ we had ___ to

do. _____ Won't for - get. ___ can't re - gret _ what I did _

___ for love... what I did for

love what I did for love. _____

# WOULDN'T IT BE LOVERLY

## from MY FAIR LADY

Lyrics by ALAN JAY LERNER
Music by FREDERICK LOEWE

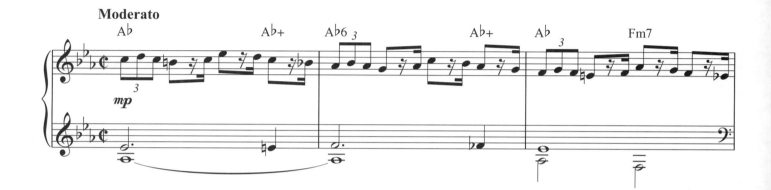

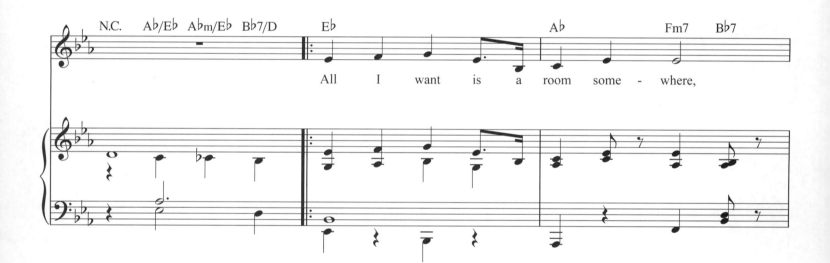

All I want is a room some-where,

Far a-way from the cold night air, With one e-

nor - mous chair; Oh, would - n't it be lov - er - ly?

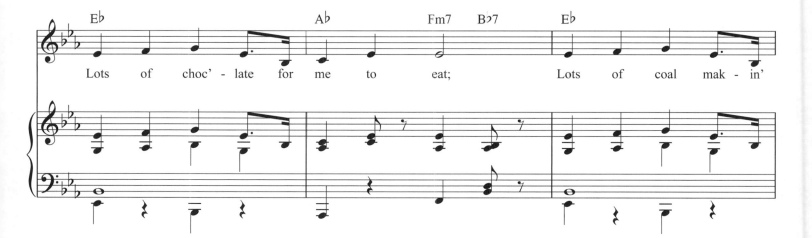

Lots of choc' - late for me to eat; Lots of coal mak - in'

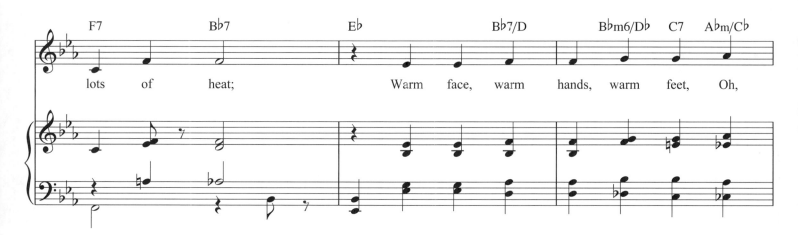

lots of heat; Warm face, warm hands, warm feet, Oh,

would - n't it be lov - er - ly? Oh, so

lov - er - ly sit - tin' ab - so-bloom - in' - lute - ly still!

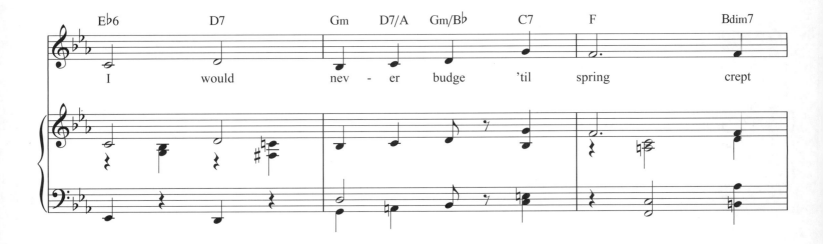

I would nev - er budge 'til spring crept

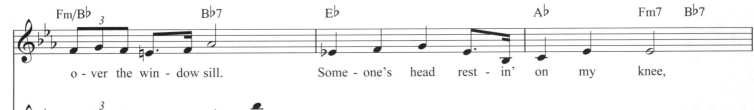

o - ver the win - dow sill. Some - one's head rest - in' on my knee,

Warm and ten - der as he can be; Who takes good

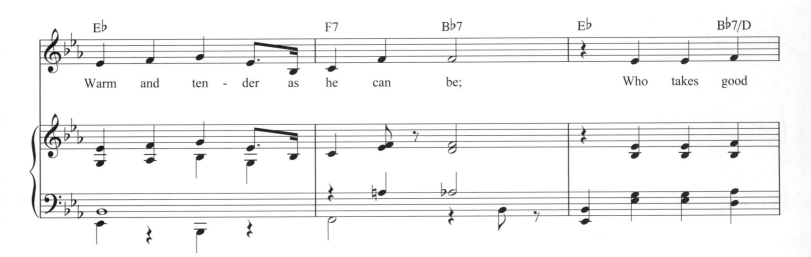

# YOU'LL NEVER WALK ALONE

## from CAROUSEL

Lyrics by OSCAR HAMMERSTEIN II
Music by RICHARD RODGERS

* alternate lyric: hold your head up high

230

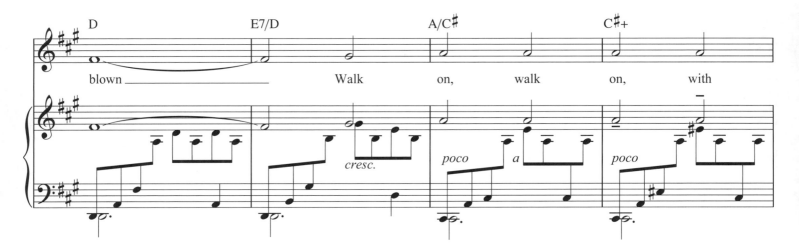

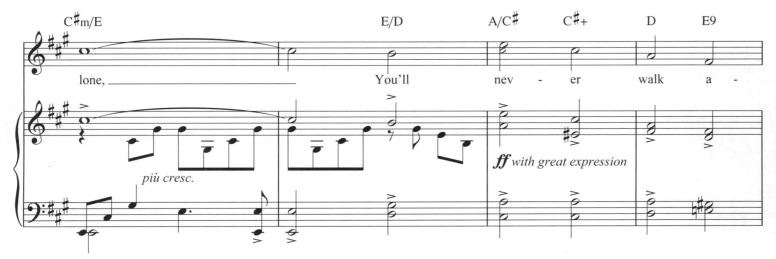

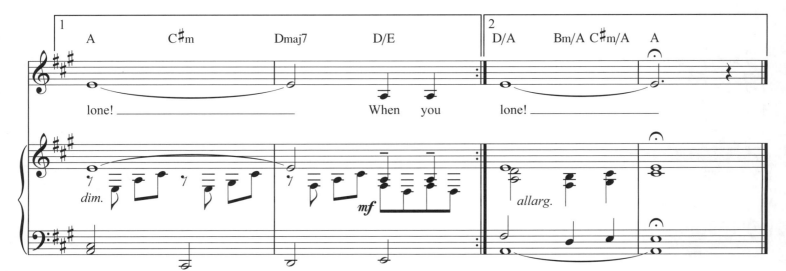

# HAL LEONARD:
## Your Source for the Best of Broadway

### THE BEST BROADWAY SONGS EVER

Over 80 songs from Broadway's latest and greatest hit shows: As Long as He Needs Me • Bess, You Is My Woman • Bewitched • Comedy Tonight • Don't Cry for Me Argentina • Getting to Know You • I Could Have Danced All Night • I Dreamed a Dream • If I Were a Rich Man • The Last Night of the World • Love Changes Everything • Oklahoma • Ol' Man River • People • Try to Remember • and more.
00309155 Piano/Vocal/Guitar ..................................$24.99

### THE BEST SHOWTUNES EVER

This show-stopping collection features over 70 songs that'll make you want to sing and dance, including: Ain't Misbehavin' • Aquarius • But Not for Me • Day by Day • Defying Gravity • Forty-Second Street • It's De-Lovely • Lullaby of Broadway • On My Own • Over the Rainbow • Send in the Clowns • Singin' in the Rain • Summertime • Whatever Lola Wants (Lola Gets) • and more.
00118782 Piano/Vocal/Guitar ..................................$19.99

### THE BIG BOOK OF BROADWAY

This edition includes 70 songs from classic musicals and recent blockbusters like *The Producers*, *Aida* and *Hairspray*. Includes: Bring Him Home • Camelot • Everything's Coming Up Roses • The Impossible Dream • A Lot of Livin' to Do • One • Some Enchanted Evening • Thoroughly Modern Millie • Till There Was You • and more.
00311658 Piano/Vocal/Guitar ..................................$19.99

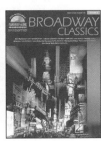

### BROADWAY CLASSICS
PIANO PLAY-ALONG SERIES, VOLUME 4
This book/CD pack provides keyboardists with a full performance track and a separate backing track for each tune. Songs include: Ain't Misbehavin' • Cabaret • If I Were a Bell • Memory • Oklahoma • Some Enchanted Evening • The Sound of Music • You'll Never Walk Alone.
00311075 Book/CD Pack.........................................$14.95

### BROADWAY MUSICALS SHOW BY SHOW 2006-2013

31 shows are covered in the latest addition to this unique series, which showcases Broadway's biggest hits year-by-year and show-by-show. A sampling of the shows covered include: Spring Awakening (2006) • In the Heights (2008) • The Addams Family (2010) • The Book of Mormon (2011) • Once (2012) • A Gentleman's Guide to Love and Murder (2013) • and many more.
00123369 Piano/Vocal..........................................$19.99

### BROADWAY SONGS

Get more bang for your buck with this jam-packed collection of 73 songs from 56 shows, including *Annie Get Your Gun*, *Cabaret*, *The Full Monty*, *Jekyll & Hyde*, *Les Misérables*, *Oklahoma* and more. Songs: Any Dream Will Do • Consider Yourself • Footloose • Getting to Know You • I Dreamed a Dream • One • People • Summer Nights • The Surrey with the Fringe on Top • With One Look • and more.
00310832 Piano/Vocal/Guitar ..................................$14.99

### DEFINITIVE BROADWAY

142 of the greatest show tunes ever, including: Don't Cry for Me Argentina • Hello, Dolly! • I Dreamed a Dream • Lullaby of Broadway • Mack the Knife • Memory • Send in the Clowns • Somewhere • The Sound of Music • Strike Up the Band • Summertime • Sunrise, Sunset • Tea for Two • Tomorrow • What I Did for Love • and more.
00359570 Piano/Vocal/Guitar ..................................$24.99

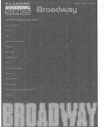

### ESSENTIAL SONGS: BROADWAY

Over 100 songs are included in this top-notch collection: Any Dream Will Do • Blue Skies • Cabaret • Don't Cry for Me, Argentina • Edelweiss • Hello, Dolly! • I'll Be Seeing You • Memory • The Music of the Night • Oklahoma • Seasons of Love • Summer Nights • There's No Business like Show Business • Tomorrow • and more.
00311222 Piano/Vocal/Guitar ..................................$24.99

### FIRST 50 BROADWAY SONGS YOU SHOULD PLAY ON THE PIANO

50 simply arranged, must-know Broadway favorites are featured in this collection of easy piano arrangements. Includes: All I Ask of You • Cabaret • Consider Yourself • Don't Cry for Me Argentina • Edelweiss • Getting to Know You • Hello, Dolly! • I Could Have Danced All Night • I Dreamed a Dream • Memory • Oh, What a Beautiful Mornin' • Ol' Man River • Sunrise, Sunset • Tomorrow • and more.
00150167 Easy Piano ................................................$14.99

### KIDS' BROADWAY SONGBOOK

An unprecedented collection of songs originally performed by children on the Broadway stage. Includes 16 songs for boys and girls, including: Gary, Indiana (*The Music Man*) • Castle on a Cloud (*Les Misérables*) • Where Is Love? (*Oliver!*) • Tomorrow (*Annie*) • and more.
00311609 Book Only..............................................$16.99
00740149 Book/Online Audio..................................$24.99

### THE OFF-BROADWAY SONGBOOK

42 gems from off-Broadway hits, including *Godspell, Tick Tick... Boom!, The Fantasticks, Once upon a Mattress, The Wild Party* and more. Songs include: Always a Bridesmaid • Come to Your Senses • Day by Day • Happiness • How Glory Goes • I Hate Musicals • The Picture in the Hall • Soon It's Gonna Rain • Stars and the Moon • Still Hurting • Twilight • and more.
00311168 Piano/Vocal/Guitar ..................................$19.99

### THE TONY AWARDS SONGBOOK

This collection assembles songs from each of Tony-winning Best Musicals through "Mama Who Bore Me" from 2007 winner *Spring Awakening*. Songs include: Til There Was You • The Sound of Music • Hello, Dolly! • Sunrise, Sunset • Send in the Clowns • Tomorrow • Memory • I Dreamed a Dream • Seasons of Love • Circle of Life • Mama, I'm a Big Girl Now • and more. Includes photos and a table of contents listed both chronologically and alphabetically.
00311092 Piano/Vocal/Guitar ..................................$19.95

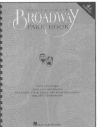

### THE ULTIMATE BROADWAY FAKE BOOK

Over 700 songs from more than 200 Broadway shows! Songs include: All I Ask of You • Bewitched • Cabaret • Don't Cry for Me Argentina • Edelweiss • Getting to Know You • Hello, Dolly! • If I Were a Rich Man • Last Night of the World • The Music of the Night • Oklahoma • People • Seasons of Love • Tell Me on a Sunday • Unexpected Song • and more!
00240046 Melody/Lyrics/Chords............................$49.99

Prices, contents, and availability subject to change without notice.
Some products may not be available outside the U.S.A.

Get complete songlists and more at **www.halleonard.com**

1216